DATE DUE

DE ~~19~~ AC~~1 03~~			
AP 28 98			
MY 28 98			
OV 25 99			
JY 28 99			
DE 6 09			
JE 1 000			
OC 9 00			
DE 5 00			
MR 29 01			
AG 01			
MY 23 02			
NO 25 02			
DE 20 02			

DEMCO 38-296

THE MALTREATED CHILD

If a better world is to be tomorrow
—it will come through the hope
and future of today's children.

THE MALTREATED CHILD

The Maltreatment Syndrome in Children
A Medical, Legal and Social Guide
Fifth Edition

By

VINCENT J. FONTANA, M.D., F.A.A.P.

Pediatrician in Chief and Medical Director
New York Foundling Hospital Center for
Parent and Child Development
Professor of Clinical Pediatrics
New York University College of Medicine
New York, New York

and

DOUGLAS J. BESHAROV, J.D., LL.M.

Founding Director
United States National Center of
Child Abuse and Neglect
Washington, D.C.
Resident Scholar at the
American Enterprise Institute for Public Policy Research

with a Foreword by

Mother Loretto Bernard
Mother General
Sisters of Charity of New York

CHARLES C THOMAS • PUBLISHER
Springfield • Illinois • U.S.A.

Distributed Throughout the World by

C THOMAS · PUBLISHER

© *1964, 1971, 1977, 1979 and 1996 by* CHARLES C THOMAS · PUBLISHER

ISBN 0-398-06547-0 (cloth)
ISBN 0-398-06548-9 (paper)

Library of Congress Catalog Card Number: 95-30664

First Edition, 1964
Second Edition, 1971
Third Edition, 1977
Fourth Edition, 1979
Fifth Edition, 1996

With THOMAS BOOKS *careful attention is given to all details of manufacturing
and design. It is the Publisher's desire to present books that are satisfactory as to their
physical qualities and artistic possibilities and appropriate for their particular use.*
THOMAS BOOKS *will be true to those laws of quality that assure a good name
and good will.*

Printed in the United States of America
SC-R-3

Library of Congress Cataloging-in-Publication Data

Fontana, Vincent J.
    The maltreated child : the maltreatment syndrome in children : a
medical, legal, and social guide / by Vincent J. Fontana and Douglas
J. Besharov ; with a foreword by Mother Loretto Bernard. — 5th ed.
        p.   cm.
    Includes bibliographical references (p.   ) and indexes.
    ISBN 0-398-06547-0 (cloth). — ISBN 0-398-06548-9 (paper)
    1. Child abuse.   2. Child abuse—Prevention.   I. Besharov,
Douglas J.   II. Title.
HV713.F6   1995
362.7'6—dc20   95-30664
                                                        CIP

This Fifth Edition is dedicated to the memory of
C. Henry Kempe and Ray E. Helfer,
pioneers in the prevention and treatment of child abuse.

To
Sister Mary Irene FitzGibbon
First Superior of the New York Foundling Hospital,
whose faith, vision and indomitable courage
laid the foundation of the great institution
in which the Sisters of Charity of New York
for over a century have lavished love and motherly care
upon more than 200,000 abandoned, neglected
or maltreated infants and children.

FOREWORD

It is a tragic commentary on the mental and moral health of our nation that one of the most common causes of childhood deaths today is physical abuse of children by their own parents. This shocking revelation, like the murder of our President and the racial bitterness that threatens civil war, should disturb our social conscience and prompt vigorous, intelligent action.

In *The Maltreated Child*, Dr. Vincent J. Fontana, Pediatrician in Chief and Medical Director of the New York Foundling Hospital Center for Parent and Child Development, analyzes the situation and outlines his work in abuse detection and therapy. Dr. Fontana has secured legislation in New York State that will rescue children from life-threatening home environments. As he phrases it: "We fail with leukemia; we fail with Hodgkins Disease; but this is one childhood disease that is in our power to conquer. And conquer it we will."

Every age has its men of vision and dedication. For more than a century, the selfless collaboration of men like Dr. Fontana has been the inspiration of the Sisters of Charity of New York in their difficult work of rehabilitating "battered children" in their hospitals and child-care homes. Never has this collaboration been more needed, more sustaining or more appreciated than it is today.

MOTHER LORETTO BERNARD
Mother General
Sisters of Charity of New York
1964

PREFACE TO THE FIFTH EDITION

Despite a quarter of a century's progress in recognition, reporting and treatment, the reports of child maltreatment in this country continue to escalate at a rate of 10 to 15 percent each year. In addition to increased public and professional awareness, the indicators of social and family breakdown feed into the statistics of child abuse and neglect. Child abuse always manifests itself with the stamp of contemporary social ills that include increases in divorces and separations, increases in adolescent pregnancies, growth of a social and economic underclass, homelessness, and the devastating effects of "crack," cocaine, and alcohol.

In 1991, after thoroughly studying the facts and figures on child maltreatment, the United States Advisory Board on Child Abuse and Neglect concluded that the child abuse problem in America represented a national emergency. In the same year the National Committee on Children reported that one in five children in this country lives in poverty, one in twelve is born to an unwed teenage mother, one in four children is reared in a single parent family, and a half million children drop out of school each year. Add to these statistics the continuing rise in the suicide rate among teenagers and one can readily see that child abuse and neglect are endangering the future of our youngsters and the future of our society.

Over the last three decades as a pediatrician and child advocate, I have observed, written about and treated the horrors of child abuse. We have learned a great deal about the causes, treatment, and prevention of child abuse. However, in spite of our present knowledge, the devastation continues. Every year abuse and neglect take the lives of over four thousand defenseless children. Despite increased awareness, the passage of protective legislation and governmental declarations about the importance of children, the problem of child abuse and neglect continues to worsen. Our national child-care system, the schools, hospitals, child welfare agencies, courts, and communities are unable to protect and provide for the welfare of our children.

Child abuse must be confronted not only because it is morally repugnant but because it is the only way to prevent the corrosive and destructive effects on our society. Overwhelming numbers of juvenile delinquents, adolescent runaways and throwaways, violent criminals, sex offenders, drug addicts, prostitutes, and murderers have testified to childhood histories of battering, neglect, and exploitation.

The correlation of child maltreatment with the violent society in which we live is incontrovertible. Complacence about child maltreatment is complacence about violence. If we do not begin to work to solve the problems of child abuse, we will be forced to live with the consequences of our actions. The costs of unrecognized and untreated child abuse weigh heavily on our educational, medical, child care, and penal institutions.

Serious injury and death from child abuse and neglect can almost always be prevented by an early detection and swift intervention. Early warning signs and symptoms of trouble are always there. Abused and neglected children give off silent signals and manifest telltale signs that include an inability to concentrate and poor performance in school, a repressed personality, restless or aggressive behavior, poor skin hygiene, a dirty and unkempt appearance, inappropriate dress for inclement weather, and black and blue marks from injuries that are not rationally explained by the parents. An enlightened physician, nurse, social worker, teacher, neighbor, friend or relative must be aware that these signs portent not only physical abuse but also potentially serious emotional and sexual abuse.

This book, the first published text in the field of child maltreatment, has and will continue to influence and educate those interested in salvaging children and families hopelessly ravaged by the ills in the midst of which we live. Child abuse is everyone's business. All child care professionals are in a position to help troubled parents cope with their children, often with relatively simple suggestions and sympathetic help—all of which can be found in the chapters of this book.

VINCENT J. FONTANA

ACKNOWLEDGMENTS

I wish to express my gratitude to Sister Cecilia Schneider, Executive Director of the New York Foundling Hospital Center for Parent and Child Development, for her foresight and leadership in the development of the first Temporary Shelter for Abusing Parents in the United States. My sincere appreciation to my loyal secretary, Miss Anne Dougherty, for the many years of patient and dedicated efforts in the preparation and coordination of the manuscript. The revision and updating of this Fifth Edition could not have been possible without the secretarial and editing assistance of Fran Antonacchio.

CONTENTS

THE MALTREATED CHILD

"Mankind owes to the child—the best it has to give."

—*United Nations Charter*

"Kill not your children for fear of being brought to want."

—*Mohammed*

"Suffer the little children to come unto me and forbid them not; for of such is the kingdom of God."

—*Luke 18:16*

"In the little world in which children have their existence, whosoever brings them up, there is nothing so finely perceived and so finely felt as injustice."

—*Charles Dickens*

"We have been told that in America's children lies the strength, the hope and the future of our country. We mean all of America's children especially those forsaken babies who are innocent victims of human weakness and misfortune."

—*Francis Cardinal Spellman*

Chapter 1

HISTORICAL DATA

Child maltreatment is not a new phenomenon. It has existed since the beginning of time. The tales of children being maltreated and battered by their parents abound in myth, legend, and literature. Throughout the Bible there runs a theme of child murder and abuse, of the destruction of a first born, of a child chosen as a burnt offering to a capricious God.

But stronger than the theme of sacrifice is the theme of the child as a nuisance to be abandoned or be abused. Greeks and Romans both abandoned infants or cast them adrift on a river, consigning them to death by exposure. In past civilizations, children were deliberately mutilated by their parents so that they might better inspire sympathy and thus be more successful as beggars. In some countries today, an infant might be discarded at birth because the child is unwanted.

Infanticide as we know it—the killing of newborn infants by suffocation, drowning, exposure to the elements, or throwing out infants with the garbage—has been practiced through the centuries as a means of disposing unwanted children. In New York City in 1869, post Civil War, the abandonment of babies had reached critical proportions. New Yorkers of the times called it an epidemic: children were literally being found in the streets after having been left bundled on doorsteps or tossed into trash cans. The newspapers expressed their horror on this wave of infanticide and abandonment, demanding that something be done about it. A Sister of Charity of New York named Sister Mary Irene Fitzgibbon took up the challenge and established a haven for cast-off babies in a small brownstone at 17 East 12 Street. Sister Mary Irene and her helpers placed a little crib at the entrance of the brownstone and advertised the function of the home throughout the editorials in the *New York Times*. It was hoped and prayed for that some of the desperate mothers would decide to drop their burdens into the little crib instead of into the city's garbage cans. And it was. From the day it was put outside the brownstone, the crib was rarely empty. Within a matter of months, hundreds of children were being brought to the brownstone on 12th Street which was to provide the foundation for one of the first foundling homes in America, known today as The New York Foundling Hospital.

With the passage of years, the phenomenon of deliberate physical abuse and neglect, not a matter of infanticide or abandonment but of inflicted cruelty which had a good chance of seriously damaging or eventually killing a child, began to surface.

One of the first recorded legal challenges to the absolute rights of parents over children occurred in New York City in 1874. It involved a severely malnourished and abused nine-year-old girl named Mary Ellen Wilson. The child was chained to her bed by her stepmother. Mary Ellen had apparently been beaten often, for her body gave evidence of severe bruises in various stages of development. Mrs. Etta Wheeler, a nurse, was going about her rounds visiting the sick when her attention was called to the plight of the abused child. Etta Wheeler and a group of interested church workers appealed to Mr. Henry Bergh of the Society for the Prevention of Cruelty to Animals after being frustrated by the lack of assistance from the police and the district attorney. They stated that they could not take any legal action to remove the child from her dangerous environment. There was no law to cover such a situation and no agency with power to interfere with the rights of the parents to bring up their child in the manner of their choosing. The Society responsible for protecting animals took on the case. The weak, emaciated, and abused child was brought into court on a stretcher and a decision was made to remove her from the care of her stepmother. Mary Ellen was sent to the Sheltering Arms Children's Home. Due to the media coverage of this case and the resulting public outcry, the first Society for the Prevention of Cruelty to Children was founded in New York in 1875.

There are still countries in the modern world in which children are still being treated as pieces of parental property, to be treated, or disposed of at the parent's will. The concept of the traditional "patria potestas" is still very much with us in our ever-continuing debate of parental rights versus children's rights. The ideas and feelings reflected in these historical practices and beliefs still confuse a society which is confronted with the question of where the authority of the parents over the child ends and where the abuse and neglect begins.

Toward the end of the nineteenth century and well into the twentieth, newborn infants, toddlers, and young children were being brought into hospitals by parents who told tales of bizarre accidents to explain the multiplicity of injuries on their children's bodies. Physicians were reluctant to believe or even suspect the possibility that parents could do anything as terrible as abuse their children willfully.

It was the work of radiologists like Drs. John Caffey, Frederick Silverman, P. V. Wooley, and W. A. Evans, Jr. who first alerted pediatricians to the specific problem of child abuse in the United States. In 1946, Dr. Caffey first reported a number of cases in which infants had multiple long bone fractures and subdural hematomas. He did not, however, speculate on the causes of the trauma. In 1953, Dr. Frederick Silverman referred to physical trauma as the most common bone "disease" of infancy. In 1955, Drs. Wooley and Evans suggested that similar injuries might be caused by the children's caregivers in an "injury prone environment." In 1957, Dr. Caffey reexamined his original data and concluded that the trauma might well have been willfully perpetrated by parents. In the same year, recognizing the importance of inflicted trauma, Drs. Jones and David recommended removal of the child from the "offending environment." It took about a decade for physicians to conclude that some parents were abusing and assaulting their children. These observations, however, never crossed the bridge from scientific publications to the mass media.

Finally, in 1962, the late Dr. C. Henry Kempe and his colleagues in Denver, Colorado, investigating the causes as well as the appropriate response to physical abuse, gained medical attention with the publication of their findings in an article entitled "The Battered Child Syndrome" in the *Journal of the American Medical Association.* Dr. Kempe stated that "if the child could only speak, the physician would be quickly led to the proper diagnosis of abuse. To the informed physician the bones tell the story the child is too young or too frightened to tell." Child abuse was rediscovered — the term "battered child syndrome" piqued the imagination of mass media. As a result, articles, photo journals, and news magazines introduced child abuse to the American public. Child abuse, a once existing invisible problem, became a visible medical-social problem.

In 1963, in an article entitled "The Maltreatment Syndrome in Children" in the *New England Journal of Medicine,* the author (VJF) widened the scope of the problem with an all-encompassing description of child abuse and neglect. The battered child phenomenon was described as the last phase of the child maltreatment spectrum and that with early detection and identification of children who suffer inflicted abuse, serious battering and death could be prevented.

Awareness of the problem of child maltreatment has increased dramatically in the last several decades through extensive media exposure, professional conferences, and a multitude of publications. When the first frenzy of child abuse swept the nation in the 1970s, laws were passed in every state requiring the reporting of all suspected cases of child abuse and neglect. In 1972, the Committee on Infants and Preschool Children of the American Academy of Pediatrics issued a statement indicating that "while a great deal of study and activity has taken place with regard to the problem of the battered child and there have been some positive results, the consensus of the Committee and its consultants is that the total problem has become magnified and is uncontrolled by present methods of management."

In 1974, the federal government recognized the importance and severity of the child maltreatment problem by passing the Child Abuse Prevention and Treatment Act, PL 93-247, which established the United States National Center of Child Abuse and Neglect (NCCAN) in Washington, D.C. The center has the responsibility with the Department of Health and Human Services (DHHS) for addressing the problem of child maltreatment, by supporting and conducting research, establishing a national collection and analysis program, providing demonstration grants and disseminating information to assist states in the development and operation of child abuse treatment and prevention programs. During the last three decades a variety of treatment and prevention programs have been developed throughout the country as a result of our more complete knowledge of the psychodynamics of child abuse and the monies made available through the implementation and continuation of the Child Abuse Prevention and Treatment Act of 1974.

The Act of 1974 was reauthorized and otherwise amended by the "Child Abuse, Domestic Violence, Adoption, and Family Services Act of 1992" (P.L. 102-295). Another amendment to the Act was made by the Juvenile Justice and Delinquency Prevention Act Amendments of 1992 (P.L. 102-586).

In 1991, the United States Advisory Board on Child Abuse and Neglect declared the existence of a national child protection emergency in which hundreds of thousands of children were "being starved, abandoned, burned and severely beaten, raped and sodomized, berated and belittled." The report warned that the maltreatment problem threatens to disintegrate the nation's social fabric by "exacerbating a range of social ills." The Board further emphasized that the failure to prevent child abuse and neglect in America costs taxpayers billions of dollars each year spent in remedial programs for juvenile delinquents, hard-core criminals, urban unrest, drug abuse, severe mental illness, and family dysfunction. The board proposed in 1992 that the federal government pursue a national strategy for protecting children that is comprehensive, child-centered, family-focused, and neighborhood-based.

Chapter 2

THE "MALTREATMENT SYNDROME IN CHILDREN"

The maltreatment of children is vigorously increasing and has become one of the world's most desperate problems. The maltreatment syndrome in children must be recognized by our society regardless of social or economic background, ages or outward appearance of a child's parents. Today, under child abuse laws in the United States, whenever a case of abuse and neglect is suspected, it must be reported and investigated with all possible speed. Abuse and neglect of children are medical-social problems of major proportions that are plaguing society by killing and crippling untold numbers of defenseless children.

This maltreatment of children has been hidden medically and socially for many years. This seems to be a result of society's disbelief that such inhuman cruelties could willfully be inflicted upon children. Some physicians have not diagnosed these cases due to lack of knowledge and/or a desire to protect their patient from any stigma or embarrassment based on mere suspicion. There are also physicians who have not reported such cases, based on fear of a court appearance or any future legal entanglements involving malpractice suits. In the last decade, however, medical schools, practicing physicians, and child care professionals have shown more awareness of the problem of child abuse, as a result of publications on the subject by Kempe, Fontana, Silverman, Steele, DeFrancis, Helfer, Krugman, and others.

The maltreatment of children encompasses all forms of inflicted "hurt" to a child, physical, psychological, or sexual caused by parental abuse or neglect. The types of neglect may be physical, medical, and/or emotional. Inflicted abuse includes the physical, emotional, and sexual maltreatment of a child.

Kempe, in his report in *The Journal of the American Medical Association* in 1962, gave results of a nationwide survey of hospitals and law enforcement agencies indicating a high incidence of battered children in a one-year period. A total of 749 children were reported as being maltreated;

of this number 78 died and 114 suffered permanent brain damage. Other reports in the medical literature have referred to this problem of child maltreatment as "unrecognized trauma," "traumatic periostitis," "parent-induced trauma," and "unsuspected trauma." None of these terms fully describe the true picture of this often life-threatening condition.

Kempe's term, "battered child syndrome," rediscovered child abuse and served well in the identification of a child who has been excessively abused and seriously battered. Unfortunately, it does not fully describe the true nature of this pediatric life-threatening condition. An all-encompassing term that could be more appropriately applied is that of the "maltreatment syndrome in children." A maltreated child often presents with no obvious signs of being battered but with multiple minor physical evidences of emotional, and at times, nutritional deprivation, neglect, and abuse. In these cases, an awareness and the diagnostic ability of the physician and other paramedical personnel can prevent the more severe injuries of inflicted trauma that are the significant causes of childhood deaths.

The maltreated child is often taken to the hospital or private physician with a history of "failure to thrive," malnutrition, poor skin hygiene, irritability, a repressed personality, and other signs of obvious neglect. The more severely abused children have been seen in the emergency rooms of hospitals with external evidences of body trauma, bruises, abrasions, cuts, lacerations, burns, soft tissue swellings, and hematomas. Inability to move certain extremities because of dislocations and bone fractures associated with neurologic signs of intracranial damage are additional signs of inflicted trauma. Abdominal signs and symptoms may also be present. Signs and symptoms pointing to the maltreatment syndrome of children, therefore, range from the simple undernourished infant often reported as "failure to thrive" to the "battered child"—the last phase of the maltreatment spectrum.

Diagnosis of the maltreatment syndrome is dependent on a precise history, physical examination, skeletal survey, specialized diagnostic procedures, and social service investigation. The history related by the parents is often at variance with the clinical picture and the physical findings noted on examination of the child. A high index of suspicion on the part of the physicians will assist them in their evaluation and differential diagnosis.

Maltreatment of children by parental abuse or neglect may occur at any age with an increase of incidence in children under three years of age. One parent, more often the mother, is the active abuser and the other parent, if present, passively accepts the on-going abuse of the child. The average age of the mother who inflicts the abuse on her children has been reported to be about twenty-six years, the average age of the father is thirty years. The abused child is usually the victim of emotionally crippled parents. The abusive parent appears to react to his own child as a result of past personal experiences of abuse, loneliness, lack of protection, and unwantedness. Divorce, separation, homelessness, alcoholism, unemployment, financial distress, isolation, and drug addiction play leading roles as "triggers," causing the potentially abusive parent to strike out at his or her own children during a crisis situation. The problem of child abuse does not seem to be limited to any particular economic, social, or intellectual level, race, or religion.

This inflicted violence on children, if not properly managed, leads to critical short- and long-term consequences. It is estimated that one out of every two "battered" children dies after being returned to his or her parents. Many of these battered children, if they survive and approach adolescence, begin to show signs of psychologic and emotional disturbances reported as "difficult to treat." It has been theorized that some maltreated children develop an unusual degree of hostility towards their parents and toward society in general. It would appear, therefore—although more investigative work is necessary—that the abuse and exploitation of children may well provide one of the sources of juvenile delinquency, future murderers, and the perpetrators of crime and violence in our society.

Child abuse laws are only the first step in the protection of the abused and neglected child. Reporting in itself will not help or save a child. It is what happens after the reporting that is of critical importance. A multidisciplinary network of protection needs to be developed in each community to implement the good intentions of these child abuse laws. The physician should be able to recognize signs of abuse and neglect, as well as conditions that mimic it and document the signs and symptoms so that the medical chart is satisfactory for admissible evidence in court. The physician's duty is not only to report the cases of child abuse but also to initiate steps to prevent further maltreatment. He must become intimately involved in the social and legal actions taken to protect the child and assist, if necessary, in the treatment of the parents.

Chapter 3

STATISTICS

In 1992, child protective services received child abuse and neglect reports alleging that nearly 2.9 million children were being maltreated. Professionals, including physicians, nurses, teachers, law enforcement, social workers, and child care providers accounted for nearly 52 percent of the reports; friends and family members accounted for 27 percent. The remaining reports were made by other persons in the community not identified. The National Center on Child Abuse and Neglect reported that on the analysis of data from thirty-four states for 1990 to 1993, the rate of children for whom the allegation of maltreatment had been substantiated or indicated increased from 14 per 1,000 children to 16 per 1,000 children.

As is apparent from Figure 1, taken from the Reports from the States to the National Center on Child Abuse and Neglect, the long-term trend in the rate of reporting for children is one of major growth. Trend data from 1976 to 1987 are based on data from the American Association for Protecting Children (AAPC) (1989), data from 1988 to 1989 are based on data from the National Committee for the Prevention of Child Abuse (NCPCA) (1992), and data from 1990 to 1992 are based on Summary Data Component of State Child Abuse and Neglect Statistics (SDC). The overall change since 1976 has been a growth of 33 percent, up from an estimated 10 children per 1,000 reported in 1976 to 43 children reported per 1,000 in 1992. This increase constitutes an average annual growth rate of 10 percent.

In 1993 in New York State alone, 138,394 child abuse and neglect cases were reported to the central registry, of which 52,326 emanated from the New York City area.

The increase in the number of reported cases of child maltreatment has been viewed as an epidemic of child abuse in the United States. Much of the increase in maltreatment is due to a greater awareness on the part of professionals and ordinary citizens. However, the increase in teenage pregnancies may well contribute to the overall increase in reported cass.

11

Figure 1. Trend in Child Reporting Rates.

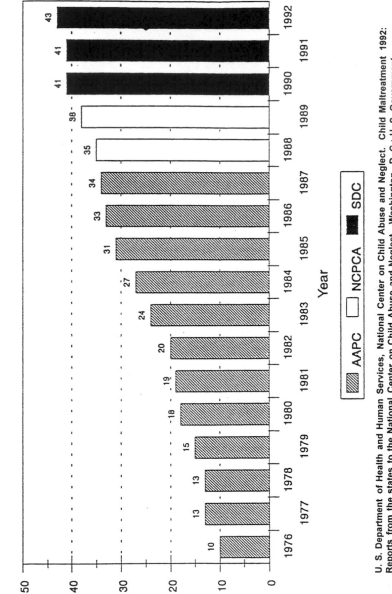

U. S. Department of Health and Human Services, National Center on Child Abuse and Neglect. Child Maltreatment 1992: Reports from the states to the National Center on Child Abuse and Neglect. Washington, D. C.: U. S. Government Printing Office, 1994.

In the period 1979 through 1988, about 2,000 child deaths were recorded annually in the United States as a result of abuse and neglect. A conservative estimate is that an average of two children die each week in New York City as a result of inflicted abuse and neglect. The most vulnerable children are those under two years of age whose parents are single or were very young at their first pregnancy. This problem has assumed critical importance in large cities with an escalating alcohol and drug addicted population. Unfortunately, child abuse fatality statistics may be underestimated because they are often not diagnosed correctly and misclassified as accidental or sudden infant death syndrome. High-risk indicators to consider in preventing death caused by abuse include a child under two years of age, in urban area, single mother, unrelated male figure in home, and a sibling in foster care. Interagency child fatality review committees that include medical examiner's office, law enforcement agency, child protective services, pediatricians with child abuse expertise, and other health and child care professionals can improve the identification of childhood deaths and the prevention of such deaths under similar circumstances. The teams also help define interagency coordination, communication, and cooperation that can improve case management efforts in child maltreatment fatalities and help distinguish Sudden Infant Death Syndrome (SIDS) from fatal child abuse.

Although physical abuse and battering of children has increased significantly over the years, child neglect is more common than any individual type of child maltreatment. Neglect has consistently accounted for approximately half of the cases of maltreatment (Figure 2). These figures may underestimate the incidence of neglect because children suffering from various forms of maltreatment are likely to be reported as abuse rather than neglect. The prevalence of psychological or emotional neglect including verbal abuse, demeaning, rejection and terrorizing a child are probably under-reported. The true occurrence of emotional abuse is difficult to determine in view of its insidious nature and standards of severity. Emotional abuse may be present in many cases of child abuse and neglect, but it may not be reported as a specific type of maltreatment.

Sexual abuse reported to child protective services has shown the largest reported increase of any form of abuse or neglect, rising from 0.7 per 1,000 children to 2.2 per 1,000 children per year in the National Incidence Studies (1980–1986).

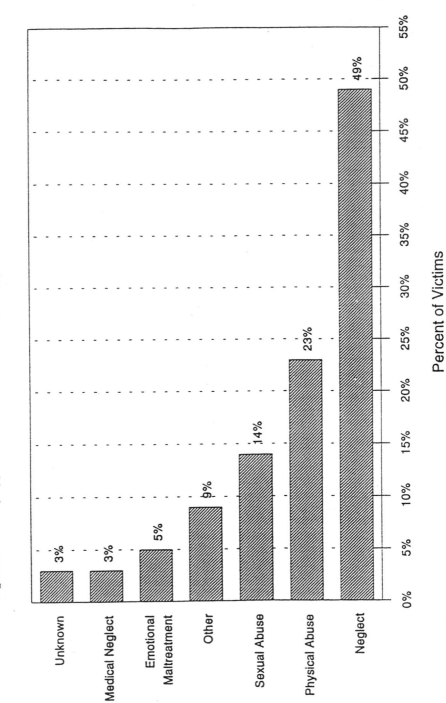

Figure 2. Victims by Type of Maltreatment (49 states reporting) (total number of victims = 918,263).

It appears that the story of the proverbial submerged iceberg is a dramatic example of the true incidence of the maltreatment syndrome in children. Reports have indicated that child maltreatment is most likely underreported and underestimated in official records. This lack of true statistics is due to a variety of factors: a portion of neglected and abused children are not taken to physicians or hospitals for attention; parents make-up believable stories and children are reluctant or too frightened to disclose what actually happened. Some physicians would rather attribute a child's symptoms to an accident or a disease rather than to actual inflicted abuse. Family court judges, many of whom are not fully informed on this problem, usually return the young victims to their parents with a light reprimand and a look of disbelief for the physician who testified in the case. In recent years, both the reluctant physician and the disbelieving judge have become more educated and aware of the seriousness and existence of child abuse.

Chapter 4

DIAGNOSIS

PHYSICAL ABUSE

An abused child is defined in family court as "child less than eighteen years of age whose parent or other person legally responsible for his or her care inflicts or allows to be inflicted upon the child serious physical injury or creates or allows to be created a substantial risk of physical injury or commits or allows to be committed against a child a sexual offense as defined in penal law."

Many of the abused children are not taken to the physician or hospital for emergency medical care until the child is in acute distress or the parents become alarmed of impending death. There are many physically abused children who are seen by physicians that go unreported or are diagnosed as accidental injury. It is therefore important in cases of maltreatment of children, that recognition and the most acute diagnostic acumen of the physician need to be utilized in order to prevent the more serious injuries resulting in the battered child syndrome.

The signs and symptoms apparent in the physical abuse of children range from soft tissue lacerations, abrasions, burns, and fractures to the more serious symptoms of coma and convulsions resulting from brain damage.

Skin

The skin is the most visible and frequently traumatized organ of the body. Soft tissue lacerations, abrasions, burns, and hematomas are common signs of physical abuse and should cast suspicion on the etiology of the presenting complaints. Even more enlightening is the presence of healed or scab-covered old abrasions or contusions of the skin in various stages of healing. Manifestations of multiple vitamin deficiencies may also be evident in these children. The inflicted skin damage can be the result of a human bite, belt buckle, coat hanger, looped cord, paddle,

16

hairbrush, iron hair curler, spoon, or whip used to punish or discipline a child. The diagnosis is easily made by noting the configuration of the bruise mark which is in the shape of the object used to inflict the abuse. Bruises and "black and blue" marks in various stages of discoloration are highly indicative of repeated inflicted injuries.

Human bites which are intentional are strong indicators of child abuse. The bite marks are usually seen around the genitalia and buttocks in an ovoid pattern with tooth imprints. The anterior teeth give the human bite mark its configuration. Photographs of the bite are important in documenting the size, shape, and type of bite. A dental consult can be of special help to physicians in evaluating bite marks in cases of child abuse. Human bite marks may cause ecchymosis, abrasions, and lacerations of the skin, and may be related to physical and sexual abuse. Bites produced by dogs and other animals tear flesh, whereas human bites usually compress flesh, causing contusions.

It is important to remember that a variety of skin conditions may be mistaken for evidences of child abuse. In the differential diagnosis, one must consider the possibility of Mongolian spots, Henoch-Schonlein Purpura, erythema multiforme, platelet aggregation disorders, and autoimmune diseases. In order to rule out a bleeding tendency that may mimic lesions due to child abuse, a battery of blood tests including platelet count, prothrombin time and partial thromboplastin time should be completed when considering the diagnosis of child abuse versus a blood dyscrasia.

Burns

The victim of abusive burning is usually a young child under the age of six years. In children seen with burn injuries, the patterns of burn injury can easily determine the source and mechanism of the inflicted abuse. The shape of any hot object used to burn a child will leave a pattern imprint on the skin. The more common agents used to injure a child include hair curlers, irons, hot water, cigarettes, cigars, ranges, ovens, hair dryers, and matches. Immersion burns involving the buttocks and extremities (Dunking syndrome) are associated with the parental intention of burning the child as a disciplinary measure especially in instances of a child's toilet training accident. Immersion burns are characterized by a distinct pattern delineating burned and unburned skin. Children held over bath tub of shallow hot water usually use their hands and feet in an attempt to protect their buttocks and perineum incurring burns to the distal parts of the extremities. Ovoid-shaped scald burns on the buttocks and burns with a "stocking" or "glove" pattern of sharp demarcation on an extremity are not likely to be accidental.

Inflicted tap water scalds are the most common type of nonaccidental burn injury. Random burn streaks on the side of the face, abdomen, extremities, and back usually indicate a splash injury. Cigarette burns are usually in clusters and in various stages of healing. In the early stages an infected cigarette burn may look like the circular lesions of impetigo. However, impetigious lesions usually do not scar whereas cigarette burns are deeper into the skin and leave a scar.

The physician must determine if the burn is abusive, accidental, or the result of folk medicine practices. The physician must rule out burns that may have occurred as a result of a true accident with a child coming into contact with hot home radiators, fireplaces, kerosene or oil heaters, and woodburning stoves. There is also the possibility that a burn might be the result of a unique religious or cultural practice. Southeast Asian healing practices which leave marks on the skin may be confused with abuse. Coining, the application of a hot coin to the skin is used to diminish pain or cure an illness. The burn markings in these instances can mimic abusive type burns.

In making a diagnosis of abusive burns, one or more of the following factors may be present:

1. History of physical evidences of past abuse and/or neglect.
2. Prior hospitalizations for "accidental" injuries.
3. History related as causative of the burn is at variance with the age of the child.
4. Delay in obtaining medical care.
5. Different stories as to how it happened from different members of the family.
6. Dysfunctional family.

Fractures

Falls are the most common causes of fractures and related injuries involving the proximal extremities, pelvis, thorax, and abdomen. Since it is difficult for infants to actively cause sufficient force to cause a fracture of the bone, it has been estimated that over 58 percent of fractures noted in infants less than one year of age are usually nonaccidental. The long bones of the body are most commonly affected in cases of inflicted skeletal injury. Metaphyseal-epiphyseal fractures can be diagnostic of a nonaccidental injury. Spiral fractures and epiphyseal separations are the result of rotational or torsional force applied to the extremity, whereas transverse fractures are the result of direct impact injury.

The results of bone injury may remain obscure during the first few days after the inflicted trauma since evidences of bone repair make their appearance only within weeks after the incident of the injury. When x-rays are obtained shortly after the traumatic episode, the bones may appear normal except for the presence of some soft tissue edema. Later, when the periosteal reactions take on calcium, the diagnostic bone changes on x-ray become more evident.

Rib fractures are noted in over 90 percent of abuse-related fractures in infants less than two years of age. The usual accidental falls and minor injuries encountered in infancy do not cause fractures of the ribs. A variety of studies have noted that cardiopulmonary resuscitation rarely causes "accidental" fracture of an infant's ribs. The usual mechanism for rib fractures in infants is a violent compression of the chest as the infant is shaken; for older children a direct blow to the chest area is responsible for any rib cage injury. Rib fractures are easily detected on x-ray during the healing stages when a callus becomes evident about ten to fourteen days after the injury.

A routine skeletal survey should be ordered in all infants less than two years of age whose history is inconsistent with signs of an unexplained injury. An infant less than one year of age with symptoms of neglect and deprivation should also have a complete skeletal examination that includes long bones and skull. In the evaluation of bone injury, radiographic identification must be correlated with a thorough history and comprehensive physical examination. A diagnosis of bone injury resulting from child abuse is usually dependent upon the presence of fractures that are inconsistent with the age of the child and in variance with the history given by the parents or the caregivers. The fractures are noted to be in various stages of resolution, and there are other evidences of child abuse and neglect.

The diagnosis of maltreatment of children is not an easy one to make and may cause unnecessary grief to parents if made quickly and prematurely, or based solely on suspicion. The diagnosis must be made by history and a complete physical examination—only after thorough consultation with other physicians and discussion with the social service worker investigating the case.

In the differential diagnosis, the physician must rule out medical conditions that may predispose soft bones to minor injury or may manifest bone findings that mimic inflicted skeletal trauma. These may be attributed to fractures and injuries associated with a prolonged and difficult labor in infancy. Unless the causes of the fractures or dislocations are obviously due to inflicted trauma, diseases such as scurvy, syphilis, infantile cortical hyperostosis, osteogenesis imperfecta, and infectious osteitis as well as accidental trauma must be considered and ruled out.

Skeletal injuries on x-ray examination, whether accidental or inflicted, are most frequently confused with scurvy because of the presence of ossified subperiosteal hemorrhages. In scurvy, however, there are characteristic changes which usually are diagnostic. A ground glass osteoporosis, cortical thinning, and ephipyseal ringing are prominent findings in scurvy. It is also important to remember that scurvy almost never occurs during the first five months of life when traumatic injuries are most commonly noted.

In infantile cortical hyperostosis one usually notes tender swellings deep in the soft tissues associated with cortical thickening in the skeleton. This disease is usually seen during the first three months of life. On x-ray, hyperostosis usually involves the mandible, clavicles, scapulae, ribs, and tubular bones of the extremities.

Infections, including tuberculosis and syphilis, can be ruled out by a history of infection, laboratory data indicating infection, bacteriological studies, and skin tests. During the early months of life, the bone lesions of congenital syphilis may resemble those due to battering. However, the lesions due to syphilis are usually symmetrical, and are associated with the luetic stigmata, and the disease can be confirmed by serological testing.

In osteogenesis imperfecta, the manifestations are usually generalized with evidence of the disorder present in bones throughout the body. The fractures in osteogenesis imperfecta are commonly of the shafts. The presence of multiple fractures associated with blue sclera, skeletal deformities, and of a family history of similar abnormalities usually confirms the diagnosis.

Neurologic signs, including exaggerated startle, and stretch reflex changes with retardation of development and growth, may mimic those of organic brain disease. The differential diagnosis, however, is easily made upon admission to a hospital. Functional neurological signs and symptoms rapidly disappear while the findings of organic nervous system do not.

Accidental trauma is common in children and should always be considered before making a diagnosis of inflicted injury. This consideration will oftentimes prevent faulty and unwarranted accusations of parents who bring their child to the attention of a physician.

Shaken Baby Syndrome

Unexplained fractures of the long bones of an infant warrants a further search for possible associated hidden evidence of subdural hematomas and head trauma. John Caffey, a pediatric radiologist, in 1946, first reported the frequency of subdural hematomas in infants accompanied by fractures of the long bones. He later offered the possible explanation of parental neglect and abuse as a cause of this association of symptoms. Recent studies in the neuroradiology literature highlights the shaken baby or shaken impact syndrome. Epidural, subdural, and subarachnoid hemorrhages can be life-threatening and often are discovered in infants having convulsions or are in a coma.

Physical abuse is a major cause of serious head injury in infants and it is estimated that 80 percent of deaths from head trauma under age two years are the result of nonaccidental injury. In 1974, Caffey described what has come to be known as the shaken baby syndrome. This syndrome is a serious form of child abuse associated with high morbidity and mortality. The accepted description involves a violently shaken child whose head has been subjected to a repetitive, acceleration-deceleration, whiplash-type motion which causes severe intracranial injury, often without signs of trauma. Shaken baby or shaken impact syndrome occurs when a parent or caregiver loses control because of the incessant crying of an infant or when the child is engaged in overly vigorous violent play.

The child who has suffered shaking injury is typically brought to the physician's office or the hospital emergency room, most commonly in respiratory distress, but with little or no external evidence of physical trauma. The child is always younger than two years and very likely to be younger than six months. Children of this age are susceptible to shaking injury because of the proportionally large size and weight of the head and the underdevelopment of the neck muscles. In addition, within the skull of a very young child, the subarachnoid spaces are relatively large, the vasculature is delicate, and the brain itself is soft, with less myelination than in an older child.

The initial examination, whether in the office or in the emergency room, must be thorough, based on a high index of suspicion, and carefully documented. Any findings that suggest trauma should be documented with sufficient detail and accuracy so that the record can serve as admissible evidence in court, if necessary. In the absence of a parental confession, successful prosecution relies heavily on the examining physician's findings.

A compassionate but objective attitude is essential when eliciting the history from the parents or caregivers. The diagnosis of shaken baby syndrome is most often made from the physical examination and imaging studies, rather than from the reported history or presenting complaint. The parent may claim that the child has been irritable or listless, unwilling to eat, or generally unresponsive.

A significant question is whether the child had been crying uncontrollably, because this is most often the trigger event. In some cases the child may have had a seizure with the parent reporting that the child fell. Parents rarely admit to having shaken the child, unless they say they found the child comatose in the crib and shook him or her in an effort at resuscitation. The usual attitude of parents is innocence or even indifference. Focal injuries in shaken baby syndrome are those resulting from impact and contact. Diffuse injuries result from the acceleration and deceleration caused by violent shaking and impact. Typical physical findings include bulging of the anterior fontanel and head circumference greater than the 90th percentile. There may be bruising, particularly of the upper arms or shoulders where the child was held while being shaken. Vital sign abnormalities may include bradycardia, apnea, and hypothermia. Leukocytosis may be present, although this cannot help differentiate shaking injury from an infectious process. Neurologic findings may include nuchal rigidity, posturing, seizures, or coma. The pupils may appear fixed or dilated. The respiratory distress may be unaccompanied by lower airway sounds or stridor (Table 1 summarizes these findings). This data should encourage physicians to suspect child abuse whenever a child under one year presents with brain injury and altered consciousness.

Imaging computed tomography (CT) or magnetic resonance imaging

Table 1. Shaken Baby Syndrome

The Physical findings

Apnea

Bradycardia

Bruising, especially of the upper arms or shoulders

Tense or bulging anterior fontanelle

Coma, altered consciousness

Fixed or dilated pupils

Retinal Hemorrhage

Head circumference greater than the 90th percentile for age

Hypothermia

Leukocytosis

Nuchal rigidity

Posturing

Respiratory distress unaccompanied by lower airway sounds or stridor

Seizures

Associated fractures of ribs or long bones

Subdural Hematomas and Subarachnoid

(MRI) studies of the skull will provide information crucial to the diagnosis. Findings include interhemispheric subdural hemorrhages, subarachnoid hemorrhages, and cerebral contusions, particularly in the frontal and occipital lobes. Parenchymal injury and cerebral edema resulting from damage to the cerebral arteries may also be seen. CT scan can confirm shaking when it shows acute interhemispheric subdural hematoma or cerebral contusions in the absence of external trauma. CT and MRI studies can help rule out meningitis, which is the most common misdiagnosis. Serial CT can also be useful in presenting the medical and legal aspects of the case in predicting neurologic outcome.

Fundoscopy—If there is any possibility that shaking injury has occurred, ophthalmoscopic examinations must be done. Although some ocular injuries may be visible with the direct ophthalmoscope, dilated fundoscopy is recommended. Pale retinal hemorrhages are the most common ocular findings associated with shaking injury. Retinal hemorrhages occur in over 50 percent of infants who have been shaken and rarely occur in accidental trauma of infants. Other ocular findings may include periorbital bruising, subconjunctival or vitreous hemorrhages, and even retinal detachment. These ocular injuries are most unlikely to have occurred during accidental injury and are usually detected by MRI.

Lumbar Puncture—Lumbar puncture produces grossly bloody or occasionally xanthochromic spinal fluid. Bloody spinal fluid (not resulting from the puncture trauma) strongly suggests intracranial injury. In some circumstances, such as when there is abnormal motor posturing, a fontanel tap is also performed. Once the data is collected and the diagnosis is confirmed by a multidisciplinary evaluation team, the child protective agency is notified.

The physician in charge of the case and the hospital child abuse committee must be sensitive to the seriousness of the diagnosis and the acute needs of these cases. They should recognize that a complete and thorough diagnostic evaluation is as important for these children as it is in the cause of fever of undetermined origin, diabetes, cancer, and other illnesses.

Physicians need not be experts in the management of child maltreatment, but they should not overlook or misdiagnose a case of child abuse any more than they should miss an occasional case of Wilm's tumor or lymphoma. In both situations, prompt recognition and diagnosis may be life-saving.

Visceral Trauma

It is estimated that visceral injuries resulting from abdominal trauma account for 3 to 5 percent of all injuries in physically abused children with an overall mortality rate estimated at 40–50 percent. Blunt abdominal trauma by the use of a fist, a kick, or an instrument can result in unexplained rupture of the stomach, intestines, liver, or pancreas with manifestations of an acute abdomen. The most common injuries encountered are duodenal intramural hematoma; laceration of the superior mesenteric artery; and serious damage to the spleen, bladder, and kidneys. Small bowel injury is one of the more difficult conditions to diagnose and oftentimes causes significant morbidity and mortality. The signs of an acute abdomen in a child signal the need for an upper gastrointestinal contrast examination, ultrasonographic diagnosis, and immediate surgical and medical consultations. In some cases of abdominal injury, there may be no visible external evidences of abuse requiring that the radiologic imaging be utilized to assist the physician in making a diagnosis. A CT scan, nuclear medicine studies, x-rays, angiography, and urography are diagnostic aids in evaluating abdominal inflicted injuries.

Nonaccidental Poisoning

Children have been reported as poisoning victims more frequently in recent years due to the escalating usage of cocaine and heroin by some parents and caregivers. Eighteen percent of reported cases have been fatal. The possibility of poisoning in a child with unexplained symptoms must be considered as a possible child abuse incident. Children may be poisoned by being given psychotropic or soporific medication prescribed for the parents to alter the child's behavior, particularly incessant crying. Children have been deliberately poisoned with over-the-counter and prescription drugs, laxatives, ipecac, salt, pepper, carbon monoxide, insulin, and alcohol. Parents who intentionally poison their children may have severe marital and/or psychiatric problems or may be drug abusers. Most child poisonings are not detected because the diagnosis is not considered and therefore indicated appropriate laboratory tests to rule out poisoning are not ordered. Toxicology screening should be considered in any child with unexplained apnea, persistent vomiting, recurrent diarrhea, and unexplained neurologic signs or seizures. In some cases, the poisoning events may be attributed to the child's "accidental" ingestion or as in Munchausen syndrome by proxy, denied by the perpetrator, who is usually the mother.

Munchausen Syndrome by Proxy

The Munchausen syndrome by proxy is a rare form of child abuse that refers to a disturbed parent or guardian who repeatedly presents an elaborate, false medical history of a child's illness—an illness in the child that is simulated and/or produced by one parent in order to attract medical attention. The illnesses include seizures, hematemesis, hematuria, false temperatures, poisonings, diarrhea, and respiratory arrest. The periodic seeking of medical attention for the child by the mother usually results in undue admissions to a hospital, laboratory testing, and invasive diagnostic procedures that may prove harmful to the child. The threat of a serious complication or death of the child resulting from any unnecessary, diagnostic procedure requires that physicians be aware of the syndrome.

The child's illness is usually fabricated or exaggerated by the mother who spends a great deal of time with the child in the hospital. She is familiar with medical terminology and gives the impression that she is the only one who can care for the child. The diagnosis is dependent upon an unusual, difficult to understand medical history which cannot be confirmed by laboratory or clinical course. When a child's signs and symptoms become apparent in the presence of the perpetrator, one should seriously consider a diagnosis of Munchausen syndrome.

In most cases studied, the mother was the perpetrator and the father was not aware of the mother's fabrication. Many of these mothers are described as "normal" or without any major psychiatric illness. The mothers involved in the syndrome thrive in a medical environment developing a familiarity with medical personnel. The motivation of these mothers may be to get attention.

Although Munchausen syndrome by proxy is uncommon, the overall mortality rate of children victims of the syndrome is 9 percent. It is therefore important that primary care physicians be aware of the syndrome, integrate collected data, request and review subspecialty consultations in order to include or exclude a fictitious illness.

SEXUAL ABUSE

Sexual abuse of children is a growing problem. In 1993, there were 330,000 reports of child sexual abuse reported to the child protective agencies in the United States. The number of children being sexually abused has risen faster in recent years than the reported cases of other forms of child abuse and neglect. The number of reported incidents has escalated as a result of a more informed medical community, greater public awareness, and school programs that teach children prevention and disclosure of sexual abuse incidents. Even with the increase in public and professional awareness of the problem, there still remains a serious underreporting. Accurate reporting of child sexual abuse has been hampered by the stigma and guilt associated with the exposure and failure of professionals to better recognize the seriousness and extent of the problem. A heightened awareness of the possibility of child sexual abuse by physicians and child care professionals can result in early effective intervention that can prevent the injustices being perpetrated on these children. Since sexual abuse is not easily identifiable as is physical abuse with its bruises, welts, and fractures, knowing what to look for and how to approach the family and victim are essential.

Approximately 75 percent of sexually abused children are female. Although it is estimated that 25 percent reported abuse victims are male, some authorities feel it is a low estimate. Boys may be reluctant to disclose their sexual abuse for fear of being labeled homosexual. In addition, the physical findings of sexual abuse in the male are not as obvious and would not be discovered on a routine physical examination. In 80 percent of the sexual assault and abuse cases, the offender is not a "stranger" but is known to the victim. Parents, parent substitutes, and relatives are found to be the most likely abusers in more than 50 percent of the reported child sexual abuse cases. In other cases, caretakers such as babysitters, child care workers, coaches, and teachers may be involved, and their average age is about thirty.

Father-daughter incest is the type most commonly reported to authorities. Mother-son incest is believed to be rare. Incest between father and son is also thought to be uncommon. Although conclusive evidence is lacking, sexual contact between brother and sister is believed by some authorities to be a common form of incest.

Child sexual abuse is a planned phenomenon in which the perpetrator is someone known to the child, having access to the child, and perpetrating the sexual act in private. Frequently, the child is pressured through the offender's position of dominance into engaging in sexual activities that the child does not understand and having child believe that the sexual activity is something to be enjoyed. The approach is usually nonthreatening, presenting the sexual activity as a game—the adult conveying to the child, "this is OK." There may be rewards for the act and usually no violence, force, or injury is involved. The abuse is usually not an isolated incident but a pattern that may continue for months or years.

In father-daughter incest, the most frequently reported for intrafamilial sexual abuse, the mother's involvement may vary from a complete lack of knowledge to an unconscious denial or willful ignorance. In some cases the mother will become a part of the involved triad by acting as an accomplice to the sexual abuse. Whether the mother's denial is deliberate or not, she plays the role of the "passive" abuser allowing the child to be assaulted by the "active" abuser. Within the incestuous family there is often to be found a broad spectrum of child maltreatment incidents, disorganization, marital problems, sexual difficulties between parents, antisocial behavior, involvement with law enforcement agencies, and substance abuse. The abusive parents may have experienced emotional or physical deprivations during their own childhood. In these parents the threat of a family breakup only intensifies their stress and inhibitions, making it less likely that the case will be reported.

The general definition of child sexual exploitation includes any act committed by an adult which is designed to stimulate a child sexually, or an act in which the child is used for sexual stimulation of an adult to which they cannot give consent by virtue of age. The sexual exploitation of a child includes the following acts:

1. Genital, oral, or anal intercourse, either attempted or completed.

2. Penetration of the oral, vaginal, or anal orifices with an object or an attempt to do so.

3. Touching the child's genitals, breasts, or nipples for self gratification.

4. Exhibitionism or inducing the child to touch the genitals of an adult.

5. Preparing, training, or exhibiting children for sexual exploitation and pornographic purposes.

6. Forcing a child to witness sexual acts for purposes of providing adult gratification.

It is not necessary for hymenal penetration or rupture to occur in order to make a diagnosis of sexual child abuse. Vaginal inflammation, tears, or discharge and evidences of sexually transmitted diseases may be the only manifestations of sexual abuse. The presence of sperm may be found outside the vagina, on the skin or around the anus as a result of the perpetrator's masturbatory action. Oral-genital sexual abuse may leave no evidences of sexual assault. In these cases, a physician's high index of suspicion and a child's story will help make the diagnosis of this hidden often unrecognized crime against children.

The consequences of child sexual abuse pose future psychological damage to the child victim of sexual exploitation. Both the short- and long-term consequences of sexual abuse are related to the age of the child, the duration of the sexual abuse, the child's relative maturity, the child's relationship to the offender, the degree of force or violence associated with the assault, the family's reaction to the offense, and last but not least, the emotional impact of the legal process. It becomes apparent that the closer the offender—victim relationship, the more violent and more extended the assault, the more disorganized the home; and the longer the court process, the more likely that the child will suffer future psychological damage. Adolescent girls are acutely aware of their own sexuality, and sensitive to the community's moral attitudes. For these reasons, adolescence appears to be a time when incest can inflict the more serious damage. Adolescent victims are more likely to encounter physical force or violence as a result of their resistance to the sexual assault. As a result, they feel unprotected, guilty, worthless, and constantly at risk. Other problems encountered by sexually-abused children include changes in school behavior, sudden drop in grades, withdrawal from friends, and regression. Victims of sexual abuse can manifest self-destructive behaviors such as abuse of alcohol and drugs, prostitution, and suicide. It is important to remember that many children, being resilient, cope and survive in spite of their abuse.

Many adults with sexual dysfunction problems report having been sexually exploited during their childhood. Women who were sexually abused as children experience difficulties in marriage involving adult sexual problems from inability to achieve orgasm to a total revulsion for heterosexual relationships. Depression is the symptom most commonly reported among adults molested as children.

Diagnosis

The physician is usually the first mandated professional to have contact with a sexually-abused child and his or her family. The cases which present themselves in the hospital's emergency room require a great deal of objectivity and self-discipline on the part of the interviewing physician. In diagnosing sexual child abuse or incest, it is important that there be a high index of suspicion, accompanied by medical intervention that is sympathetic and professional. Treatment of the sexually-abused child and parents begin when the victim and parents arrive in the emergency room. The physician's approach must encompass sensitivity, empathy, and appropriate medical treatment, while at the same time giving due consideration to the emotions of the sexually-abused child, the accused perpetrator, and the multi-troubled family unit. A good patient-physician relationship is probably the most crucial factor in achieving a trusting rapport which will ensure eliciting a reliable history. Making a definitive diagnosis depends on obtaining a complete and comprehensive history, medical examination, and laboratory testing.

A complete investigative interview is best accomplished when a physician, a child protective worker, or a law enforcement official, is videotaped or audiotaped using a two-way mirror for simultaneous observation by other concerned professionals. This team effort will minimize the trauma of separate, multiple, repetitive interviews, giving each professional the opportunity to gain the information needed, and lessening the period of time spent with the victim and family. The damaging psychological effects suffered by the sexually-assaulted child are compounded frequently by the attitudes of those involved in its initial discovery and by the investigative actions that follow. The questioning of a child is an emotionally charged proceeding as is the physical examination necessary to ascertain penetration, injury, or possible evidence of genital infections. Together with the parent's possible verbal and psychological abuse, these questions and examinations intensify the emotional crisis. It is the responsibility of the physician to explain to the child and to the parents what to expect from the interrogation, the physical examination, and the treatment process.

History

Those who are responsible for medical evaluations of the sexually-abused child must recognize the critical importance of a thorough history since diagnostic physical findings of abuse are found in only 3 percent to 10 percent of child victims. The history should include a clear statement of the alleged sexual assault, physical injury, and presenting symptoms. Interviewing techniques vary with the age of the child. In questioning the child about the sexual assault, a frank, direct approach is more productive. Credibility of detailed and explicit descriptions by the child of sexual abuse can be elicited utilizing specialized interviewing skills and tools. It is necessary to communicate with the child with a vocabulary that the child understands. Using dolls during the interview can be very helpful, making it easier for the child to tell his or her story utilizing the doll's body parts. These dolls should not be used by interviewers who have not been trained in the dangers and benefits of their use, and they should never be used alone to determine whether abuse has occurred. When asking three- to six-year-old children about abuse, a child's drawings may be helpful. The professional's attitude should reflect a willingness to believe the child victim's story. Nonetheless, care must be taken to ensure the child's story is neither fantasy or lie. Teenage girls are more likely to fabricate allegations of sexual abuse than younger girls.

The patient should be encouraged to reveal all details concerning the sexual abuse incident. The physician must document the facts regarding date, time, place, and alleged perpetrator, and must be able to describe sites of sexual abuse (e.g., mouth, breasts, genitals, anus). Specific information concerning menstrual history, occurrence of penetration, and whether or not ejaculation took place should be recorded. During the interrogation procedure, the physician should be aware of certain physical and behavior indicators of sexual abuse (Table 2). Genital trauma and sexually transmitted diseases represent only one end of the spectrum of the problem. Behavioral changes and emotional reactions resulting from the sexual abuse are much more common presenting features in these cases.

The documenting of a complete medical history and physical examination are important steps in preparing for the intervention process. In addition, this information clearly written provides legal documents which may serve as evidence in future court proceedings.

Table 2. Child Sexual Abuse Indicators.

Child's Physical Indicators

 Difficulty in walking or sitting

 Torn, stained or bloody underclothing

 Pain or itching in genital area

 Vaginal discharge

 Bruises or bleeding in external genitalia, vaginal or anal areas

 Venereal disease (especially in pre-teens)

Child's Behavioral Indicators

 Unwilling to change for gym or participate in physical education class

 Withdrawal, fantasy or infantile behavior

 Bizarre, sophisticated or unusual sexual behavior or knowledge

 Problems in school

 Poor peer relationships

 Changes in eating and sleeping habits

 Delinquent or runaway

 Reports sexual assault by caretaker

Physical Examination

The physical examination usually follows immediately after the interview with the child. A medical examination is essential regardless of the date of the alleged assault. In conducting the physical examination, sensitivity to the child's feelings and a reassuring attitude are of utmost importance. The child should be told what the examination will consist of, and consent forms should be signed for all procedures and treatments. Allow a parent to stay with the child if the child wishes him or her to be present. During the examination itself, particularly the gynecological inspection, the child's need for privacy should be respected. Use appropriate gowns and drapes to ensure modesty while the child is being examined. Avoid the possibility that the physical examination could add further trauma to an already stressed and abused victim. If a child is in a disturbed mental state or in pain, it may be necessary to postpone the examination and prescribe mild sedation.

The physician should record the child's general physical appearance as well as the child's emotional, behavioral, and developmental status. A general physical examination should focus on and document any evidences of physical trauma such as hematomas, bruises, abrasions, bite marks, lacerations, or injuries to the genital area. Physical evidences of trauma should be documented by taking color photographs of the injury. The mouth should be examined for signs of trauma. A history suggesting recent fellatio may give evidences of herpetic infection or venereal disease.

The hymenal ring should be inspected documenting the presence and diameter of the opening, and the evidence of fresh tears or old scars. Findings suggestive of abuse include hymenal lacerations, transection, hymenal remnants and lacerations of the posterior fourchette. The presence of bruises around the anus, scars, anal tears, and anal dilation are important indicators of sexual abuse. Colposcopic examination can be very helpful in obtaining a detailed magnified inspection of the genitalia in a search for the physical signs of sexual abuse.

Laboratory tests for semen are necessary to substantiate incest or rape. The incidence of sexually transmitted diseases among abused children is approximately 10–15 percent. Laboratory procedures should include endocervical, pharyngeal, and rectal cultures to ascertain the possible existence of sexually transmitted diseases such as gonorrhea, syphilis, or genital herpes. The presence of certain sexually transmitted diseases such as condylomata, chlamydia, HIV infection, and genital herpes can be transmitted nonsexually. These diseases can be contracted in utero, perinatally, or accidentally.

Caution must be exercised since some physical findings previously thought to result from sexual abuse may well be present in "nonabused" children. It is also important to be aware that other conditions which may mimic sexual abuse include masturbation, congenital hemangiomas, streptococcal infection, accidental perineal injuries, and congenital vaginal or anal anomalies. Bruising of the skin and genital ecchymosis may be seen in patients with lichen sclerosis, a vulvar dystrophy which occasionally affects the genitalia of young children. Vulvar irritation is commonly seen in small children as a result of poor skin hygiene. Wetness of diapers or scratching can cause maceration of the perineal area and local infections. When a child less than twelve years of age is pregnant or has contracted a venereal disease, there is reasonable cause to suspect child sexual abuse.

Treatment

The physician should institute appropriate medical treatment for injuries and administer specific antimicrobial therapy dependent on positive laboratory results for sexually transmitted diseases or prophylaxis dependent on individual circumstances.

If the child has been severely injured or a continuous dangerous situation exists for the child, hospitalization is indicated. Every hospital should have established protocols for taking children into protective custody.

After completion of the examination the physician should meet with the parents to explain the findings and any medical recommendations and follow-up services. It is also an opportunity for answering any questions the parents might have. Since all cases of suspected child sexual abuse involve civil as well as criminal offenses, parents should be informed of the state child abuse law reporting requirements. Physicians are mandated by law to report to child protective services whenever they suspect that a child has been sexually abused. The physician should be familiar with the process of reporting child abuse and neglect to the appropriate child protective agency in the community. When the report is made, the physician should give an opinion as to whether or not sexual abuse has occurred. Frequently, making a definitive diagnosis of child sexual abuse is a difficult one because the physical findings are inconclusive, and the history obtained unreliable. The state child abuse reporting laws do not require that physicians determine who committed the abuse or whether the offense was definitely committed. The state reporting laws require only that physicians report their *suspicions* of any child abuse incident that comes to their attention. Since all state laws require physicians and other mandated health personnel to report to child protective agencies any *suspected* case of sexual assault on a child, hospitals should develop a protocol for reporting, examining, and treating of all suspected child sexual abuse cases. Hospital emergency rooms should have administrative policy prominently displayed for the medical staff. The Committee on Child Abuse and Neglect of the American Academy of Pediatrics has issued "Guidelines for the Evaluation of Sexually Abused Children." Physicians should be aware of this statement.

Child abuse cases can never be handled effectively by a single individual. The intervention in a sexual abuse case requires a team approach. It is critical to involve the nursing staff, physician, a social worker, a child protective worker, mental health professional, and a law enforcement official early in the management process. Each discipline will approach the problem from a different perspective, but all will play equally important roles in protecting the child and providing a multidisciplinary intervention that is critical to the effective management and treatment of child sexual abuse.

The dynamics of child sexual abuse are such that the family members and participants in the sexual act rarely ask for help. Self-reporting often brings with it further family disruption, loss of a financial provider, social stigma, and the likely incarceration of the perpetrator. We must therefore accept the fact that these are in most cases not motivated clients wanting help. Treatment for child sexual abuse, therefore, is not easy and represents unique difficulties for professionals. We do not have complete or final answers to the question of how to treat sexual abuse effectively. We do know, however, that interdisciplinary communication and coordination will bring us closer to making progress in strengthening the family unit and hopefully helping the child to remain in a safe and healthy environment. Although not every child will need treatment, every child should be assessed for mental health difficulties and if there is need, treatment as indicated.

Giarretto has promoted the value of a specialized multifocal program for incestuous families. The treatment process includes individual treatment for members of the triad; mother-daughter counseling, marital therapy; father-daughter counseling; family treatment; and coordination with community agencies such as Alcoholics Anonymous, Al-Anon, Parents Anonymous, and Parents United. Therapy to the troubled family must be long-term and supportive and must extend beyond dealing only with the immediate crisis.

The immediate objective in sexual abuse cases is to prevent the continued exploitation of the child. This may require hospitalization or removal from the home and placement in a foster home. In situations where the perpetrator is not motivated or amenable to treatment, a coordinated collaboration with the justice system can provide the alternative to treatment, namely, prosecution and imprisonment.

In summary, the problem of sexual abuse is in urgent need of professional recognition and the establishment of coordinated multidisciplinary programs of prevention, intervention, and treatment. This can only come about through a better informed, more concerned, and more sympathetic medical and child care community. The physician should act as an advocate for the child if court proceedings ensue, and encourage the appointment of a guardian ad litem to represent the child's best interests in court. At the same time, the task of protecting the child victim cannot be the sole responsibility of any one individual since no single strategy can meet the complex needs of these children and their families. Thus, there must be a coordinated, cooperative effort by individual professional services designed to meet the medical, social, psychological, and legal needs of these incestuous families. Only in this way will we be able to prevent future child sexual abuse in the community and reduce the social isolation, family disruption, and the hurt experienced by the child victim.

EMOTIONAL ABUSE

Emotional abuse of children is the most insidious form of maltreatment which results in the impaired psychological growth and development of children. Most forms of emotional maltreatment are very subtle and are usually overlooked especially in the presence of physical abuse and neglect. It has not received proper attention because emotional or verbal abuse leaves no physical marks, whereas physical abuse often leaves obvious physical signs and scars. It includes the continued demeaning rejection, intimidation, or humiliation of a child. A parent using words that "hit as loud as a fist" is the verbal assault of a child which damages a child's sense of self-esteem and well-being. It is the withholding of love and affection which allows a child to feel unwanted.

Most emotional abuse occurs for many of the same reasons that physical abuse occurs. Parents feel isolated, under stress, drug or alcohol addicted, and unable to cope. A lack of parenting skills, unrealistic expectations of children, and an inability to love and empathize can lead to both emotional and physical abuse.

Emotional abuse of children takes its toll on its victims. Many of these children experience a sense of estrangement, alienation, depression, and self-deprecation. These characteristics oftentimes lead to difficulties in school and antisocial behavior. Because of this subtle form of abuse, with low self-esteem and a feeling of isolation, the victim child may turn to alcohol and drugs for escape and even attempt suicide. They often end up as the runaways, the throw-aways, and the kicked-out kids living in the streets.

If not properly managed, this distorted relationship between parents and children can be life-threatening with profound consequences to the child, family, and society which are both immediate and long-term. As a result, we are faced with the prospect of thousands of children growing up unhappy, maltreated, deprived, and suicidal. The teenage delinquents, alcoholics, drug addicts, and prostitutes on our streets are for the most part products of a multitroubled violent home environment in which they were the victims of inflicted abuse and neglect. These are the children who assault, rob, and murder. There are thousands of such troubled, emotionally damaged youths who are finding it difficult to live with or without their parents. Normal lines of communication between these parents and their children are nonexistent and have been replaced by harsh words, unfair punishment, and physical abuse which intensifies and perpetuates a vicious cycle of violence breeding violence from one generation to the next.

CHILD NEGLECT

In the wide spectrum of commissions and omissions by parents and guardians, the broad term "neglect" has come to include emotional neglect, physical neglect, malnutrition or failure to thrive, inappropriate clothing, lack of supervision, medical neglect, educational neglect, and abandonment (Table 3). In all these cases, inadequate parenting is the

Table 3. Types of Child Neglect.

1. Abandonment—totally or for long periods of time.
2. Lack of supervision—young children left unattended at home or in the care of other children too young to protect them.
3. Lack of adequate clothing and poor personal hygiene—severe diaper rash, dirty, unbathed, pediculosis.
4. Lack of medical or dental care—unmet health needs, lack of immunizations and dental care.
5. Lack of adequate nutrition—insufficient quantity and quality of food resulting in severe developmental lags or "failure-to-thrive."
6. Lack of adequate shelter—dangerous and unsanitary housing conditions.
7. Lack of emotional stimulation—physical and mental retardation syndromes and/or "failure-to-thrive."
8. Lack of education-chronic absenteeism

major issue with a failure to perform parental duties, including those of supervision, nurturing, and protection. Medical neglect results when parents delay seeking medical or surgical treatment for a seriously ill child, or they may simply ignore a child's general medical care by not securing the necessary childhood immunizations or dental care. Children may be deprived of adequate food, clothing, and shelter leading to ultimate abandonment. General neglect of a child may be manifested in the appearance of a severe diaper rash, poor skin hygiene, excessive hunger, dehydration, and malnutrition.

The mothers or caregivers may be consumed by the misuse of drugs or alcohol, social problems, inner conflicts, and environmental stress creating severe depression, apathy, and inability to care and nurture the child. These neglectful mothers often lack self-esteem as the result of their own childhood neglect having never developed the capacity for mothering and giving affection.

In chronically neglectful families, the child exists within an environment of family disorganization and isolation. Children reared in this type of environment are at risk in matters of health, education, security, and normal development.

The dilemma of determining whether a child has been abused is difficult enough; to determine when a neglect report must be made is even more difficult, especially in cases of emotional neglect. Child neglect can be more serious than abuse. Physicians and child care workers should be aware of the physical and behavioral indicators of parental neglect of children (Table 4).

Table 4. Indicators of Parental Neglect of Children.

Child's Physical Indicators

- Consistent hunger, poor hygiene, inappropriate dress
- Consistent lack of supervision, especially in dangerous activities or long periods
- Unattended physical problems or medical or dental needs
- Abandonment
- Often tired or listless

Child's Behavioral Indicators

- Begging or stealing food
- Extended stays in school (early arrival and late departure)
- Attendance at school infrequent
- Constant fatigue, listlessness, or falling asleep in class
- Alcohol or drug abuse
- States there is no caretaker

Parent's Behavioral Indicators

- Misuses alcohol or drugs
- Has disorganized, upsetting home life
- Is apathetic, feels nothing will change
- Is isolated from friends, relatives, neighbors
- Has long-term chronic illness
- Cannot be found
- Has history of neglect as a child
- Exposes child to unsafe living conditions
- Evidences limited intellectual capacity

Parents or child caregivers unwilling or unable to provide necessary nurturance, stimulation, encouragement, and protection to the child at various stages of development inhibits the child's normal growth and development. The results of emotional neglect are also observable in the child's behavior, social and educational conduct (Table 5).

Maternal Deprivation Syndrome

A particularly serious form of neglect involves the prolonged emotional deprivation of a child by a parent resulting in failure to thrive or

Table 5. Indicators of Emotional Neglect of Children.

Child's Physical Indicators

- Exhibits one or more of the following:
- Speech disorders
- Lags in physical development
- Failure to thrive

Child's Behavioral Indicators

- Habit disorders (sucking, biting, rocking, etc.)
- Conduct disorders (antisocial, destructive, etc.)
- Neurotic traits (sleep disorders, speech disorders, inhibition of play)
- Psychoneurotic reactions (hysteria, obsessions, compulsions, phobias, hypochondria)
- Behavioral extremes: compliant, passive, shy, aggressive, demanding
- Overly adaptive behavior: inappropriately adult or inappropriately infantile
- Developmental lags (mental, emotional)
- Attempted suicide

Parent's Behavioral Indicators

- Treats children in the family unequally
- Doesn't seem to care much about child's problems
- Blames or belittles child
- Is cold and rejecting
- Withholds love
- Behaves inconsistently

maternal deprivation syndrome. The term failure to thrive is not a diagnosis but purely a descriptive term that denotes a child's growth failure. The term came into being at the beginning of this century to describe the malnourished and neglected condition of babies brought to foundling asylums. These institutionalized children lacking any emotional stimulation became apathetic and anorexic resulting in their failure to gain weight and grow normally. With the advent of the recognition of child maltreatment in the early sixties, the term maternal deprivation was generated in the context of child abuse and neglect.

Mothers of failure to thrive babies are often suffering from depression and an inability to "bond" with their children. Many of these mothers have experienced sexual abuse, physical abuse or neglect during their early childhood. These mothers have difficulty in recognizing the nutritional requirements of the child and the need for medical and social help. They lack empathy and are unable to relate to their babies both physically and emotionally resulting in a child's retarded growth and development.

Failure to thrive is a symptom complex that denotes poor weight gain. It has been defined as a body weight less than the third percentile for age and gender, or a weight less than 80 percent of that expected for height and age. The terms, organic and nonorganic, have emerged in an effort to establish the causes of underdevelopment ascribed either to an underlying physiologicpathology or child neglect. In reality the common pathway leading to growth failure and undernutrition has multiple etiologies including maltreatment. Organic versus nonorganic etiologies are not mutually exclusive. The pathophysiologic causes of failure-to-thrive include a variety of endocrine, congenital and metabolic disorders, familial short stature, chronic infection, immune deficiency disorders, nutritional deficiency, and diseases involving the central nervous system, urinary and gastrointestinal tract.

A definite confirmation of etiology is dependent on a diagnostic evaluation within a hospital setting. A complete personal, family, and nutritional history and a thorough physical examination should be documented. All available lengths and weights should be recorded on a standard growth chart. Minimal laboratory examination should include a complete blood count, an erythrocyte sedimentation rate, urinalysis, thyroid testing, x-rays for bone age, sweat chlorides, and malabsorptive studies. Developmental evaluation of the child is also obtained. These studies will help differentiate and eliminate a large number of illnesses which can cause growth retardation.

Hospitalization is recommended to monitor adequate dietary intake, to observe the child's behavior and the family-child interactions. During the child's hospital stay, it is important that ongoing interactions between the mother and child be observed, assessed, and recorded. The mother's parenting knowledge base, social environmental status, and psychological state are evaluated. Marital crisis or other relationship difficulties are documented in order to develop a counseling and parent training plan to enhance mother-child "bonding" or attachment. The only way to establish an unchallengeable cause-effect relationship between the infant's inadequate nurturing and his or her symptoms is to observe significant recovery when the mothering is altered.

Once the causes of failure to thrive have been determined, it is important for social workers, physicians, psychiatrists, and other health care professionals to provide the necessary services to eliminate any disturbances in mother-infant interaction.

Several basic approaches can be used to improve the mother's parenting function: eliminate or diminish social or environmental stresses, reduce demands on the mother to a level within her capacity (through child day care placements, homemaker, baby sitter), provide emotional support, sympathy, parenting education, supportive case work, and resolve or diminish the inner psychic conflict.

With high-risk families in which children have been previously reported as failure to thrive or those documented as abused or neglected, a missed medical appointment must set in motion a prompt visit from social services or a visiting nurse service. If these services are not available, a telephone contact should be made to ascertain why the appointment was not kept and to urge a visit the next day. If appointments are not kept, a child abuse report to the child protection agency should elicit a home visit by a social worker to investigate and assess the home situation.

The future of neglected children is dependent on recognition and professional involvement. These children, if they survive their chronic neglect, can be physically and emotionally damaged. Physicians, nurses, social workers, and child developmentalists should assist child protective workers in their evaluation and management of the victim and the family.

CASE REPORTS

Case 1: The patient was born prematurely after six months' gestation. At the age of one year, she was taken to a hospital emergency room with a history of having fallen out of her crib. X-ray study revealed fractures of the right and left wrists. She was not admitted to the hospital at that time. Several weeks later, the mother took her to another hospital where she stated that she tripped with the baby and noted swelling on the ankles. Fractured right and left ankles were noted on x-ray examination.

Two months later, the patient was admitted to a third hospital with a fractured left arm and signs of malnutrition. X-ray study at the hospital revealed healed old fractures as well as the newly incurred fracture of the left humerus.

The case was referred to social service workers, who, after investigation, reported the parent's denial of having inflicted trauma and considered the home environment adequate. No further action was taken in view of the social service report.

At the age of two, this patient was admitted to the hospital with multiple fractures and symptoms strongly suggesting rickets or scurvy. The case was again studied by the social service section of the hospital and again the home environment was found acceptable. The Society for the Prevention of Cruelty to Children investigated the family problem to rule out physical abuse to the child. At that time, the mother stated that she was a victim of "epileptic seizures." The Society felt assured that the injuries sustained by the patient were due to trauma incurred during the mother's seizures and not to any negligence or abuse on the part of the parents. Six months later, the child was taken to the emergency room of a hospital where she was pronounced dead on arrival.

The mother stated that she had fallen down a flight of stairs with the child in her arms. At the time that the mother brought the patient into the emergency room, there were no signs of trauma on any part of her own body.

At autopsy, the following findings were noted: Subdural hemorrhages; cerebral edema; contusions of the scalp and face; multiple abrasions of the face and extremities, with scab formation; old lacerations of the lips; and multiple contusions and abrasions of the body. A diagnosis of maltreatment was made by the medical examiner, but no legal action was taken at the time.

Case 2: Several months later the one-month-old sibling of the patient in Case 1 was admitted to the hospital with a diagnosis of malnutrition, dehydration and possible vitamin deficiency. The patient responded well to supportive measures and was discharged in good condition.

Two weeks later examination in the pediatric follow-up clinic revealed soft-tissue swellings of the left wrist and left thigh. The patient was admitted to the hospital and x-ray study showed fractures of the distal end of the left radius and ulna. The possibility of pathologic fractures was considered, but laboratory data were all within normal limits.

Inflicted trauma was suspected and data on the medical past history of the patient and sibling were obtained. The "accidental death" report of the sibling in Case 1 prompted further investigations which confirmed the diagnosis of maltreatment in Case 2.

The parents persisted in their denials of inflicted trauma and abuse and expressed concern for the welfare of their children. The mother impressed both physicians and social service workers with her affection and care of her four children. Her clinic visits gave further evidence of her motherly affection. The children appeared well dressed, and there was no obvious indication of neglect.

In view of the past history of maltreatment in another sibling and the inadequacy of the parent's explanation of the patient's physical findings, this child was kept in the hospital to await court action. The court's decision, in view of the evidence presented, was to place the child in a foster home.

Case 3: A six-week-old infant was admitted to the hospital because of swelling of the right thigh of four day's duration. The mother stated to the examining physician that the child had fallen from its crib and struck its right leg on the floor. X-ray examination revealed complete fracture through the midshaft of the right femur with posterior displacement of the distal fragment. The patient was in Bryant's traction for two weeks and was discharged in good condition after application of a hip spica.

A few weeks later the child was admitted to another hospital with multiple contusions and abrasions. Investigation by the social service department indicated that the father had thrown the child on the floor, shattering the cast and inflicting serious head trauma resulting in bilateral subdural hematomas. The child was recently seen in the pediatric clinic, where multiple signs of intracranial damage were noted. The child is now blind and mentally retarded.

These three cases of maltreated children are typical examples of parentally inflicted trauma. In the first case, the abuse and trauma led to the patient's death. The patient in case 2 was rescued from future maltreatment and possible death by removal of the patient from the life-threatening environment. The child was placed in a foster home waiting the rehabilitation of the parents and adjustment of the home environment. In case 3, the results of a battered child, if the patient survives, are evident. This child gives evidence of the irreversible brain damage resulting from repeatedly inflicted trauma.

These cases strongly express the possibilities facing the victim of maltreatment. The results depend on the alertness and astuteness of the medical, social and legal agents of our society.

Case 4: This one-year-old male infant was born at term. His first admission was at the age of five months for anemia and an abscess formation of the right tibial area. There was no history or evidence of trauma on physical examination. The parents related a history that there were many insects and rodents at home. The patient had not received any immunization. There were four other siblings at home. There was no history of tuberculosis or allergies in the family.

On physical examination, the infant looked pale and acutely ill. He was in the 40th percentile for his weight. The most significant finding was the fluctuant erythematous swelling (3 × 4 centimeters) over the right tibia with tender right inguinal adenopathy.

X-rays of the anterior aspect of the right lower leg showed soft-tissue mass with no bony involvement. Incision and drainage under local anesthesia was done, and the child was discharged on the fifth hospital day with a weight gain of one-half pound.

The patient was readmitted at eight months of age for a hematoma of the left ear pinna and anemia. The parents stated that the swelling of the ear was the result of a rat bite. A detailed social service inquiry, including a home visit, was undertaken during the second admission. There were many family problems apparent in all areas of married family life. The social worker could shed no light on the cause of the child's hematoma or upon the abscess treated on the first admission.

A third admission was noted at one year of age for impetigo. Another extensive social service investigation was conducted. From the information gathered by the investigators, the medical suspicions and the physical findings, neglect on the part of the parents resulted in court action. This action was taken to protect the child from future recurring injuries. The child, by court action based on evidence presented, was placed in The New York Foundling Hospital.

Case 5: A five-year-old male child was admitted to the hospital for multiple contusions and abrasions about the body and head secondary to trauma. The question of inflicted trauma was entertained by the examining physicians. History revealed that the mother was responsible for the maltreatment of this patient. The father and child both confirmed the fact that the mother was responsible for the periodic episodes of abuse. The child was with foster parents from age one to four years and was living with his own parents when the injuries occurred.

On physical examination, the child had multiple areas of contusions and abrasions about the face and head, chest and extremities. Skull and total body x-rays revealed no fractures. Patient was discharged to The New York Foundling Hospital and plans were made to have the child placed in a foster home.

Case 6: An eight-year-old boy who was a ward of The New York Foundling Hospital was admitted for multiple contusions inflicted by the foster parents, as related by the child, for misbehaving at school. These periodic beatings were far beyond the normal excuses of discipline. Further questioning revealed that the foster parents would at times force the child up against a hot radiator until body burns were evident.

On physical examination, multiple contusions and ecchymosis of back and extremities were noted. Total body x-rays revealed no fractures. Patient was otherwise normal.

The child was returned to The New York Foundling Hospital for continued social service investigation and placement.

Case 7: A three-year-old male was admitted from the emergency room with burns involving 10 to 15 percent of the body surface. According to the history, the child was placed in a bathtub and hot water was turned on accidentally.

On physical examination, his temperature was 101.80, pulse 130. The examination was essentially normal except for redness and blistering of feet, buttock, scrotum and hands.

The patient was treated with antibiotics, sedatives and open air treatment with aseptic care of the burns. X-ray of the extremities and rib cage revealed no fractures; chest film was normal. CBC, urinalysis and electrolytes repeatedly were normal. After thirty-seven days of hospitalization, the child had a good recovery from the burns.

The social service department investigated the problem in depth. Both the patient and another sibling were born out of wedlock with different fathers. At the time of the alleged accident, another male companion of the mother's was left to care for the patient. During a fit of rage, this friend of the mother's placed the child in a tub of boiling water.

The areas burned aroused the suspicions of the physicians. The perineal area and buttocks were severely burned; the hands and feet were also involved. The intervening areas of the body surface were normal. It appeared from the parts of the body burned that the child was forced to sit in the boiling water and, in the patient's attempt to protect himself, he extended his feet and hands which came into contact with the water.

Social service investigations and family unit adjustments warranted discharge of this child to his home. The physician recommended periodic visits to the Pediatric Clinic and interval visits to the home by social service.

These case reports of maltreatment in children represent only a small number of the ways that abuse and neglect can be inflicted. They also illustrate the different members or individuals in a family group who can be responsible for the willfully inflicted trauma or abuse on these children.

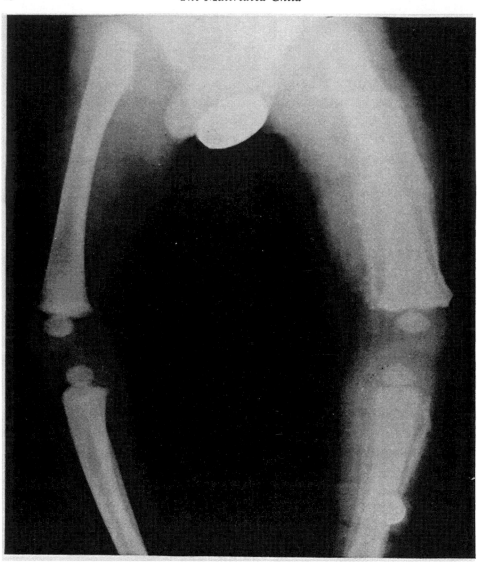

Figure 3. Female, six months old with history of thigh swelling. Film taken four to eight days after injury shows evidence of periosteal hemorrhage, metaphyseal fragmentation and periosteal reaction of femur, tibia and fibula.

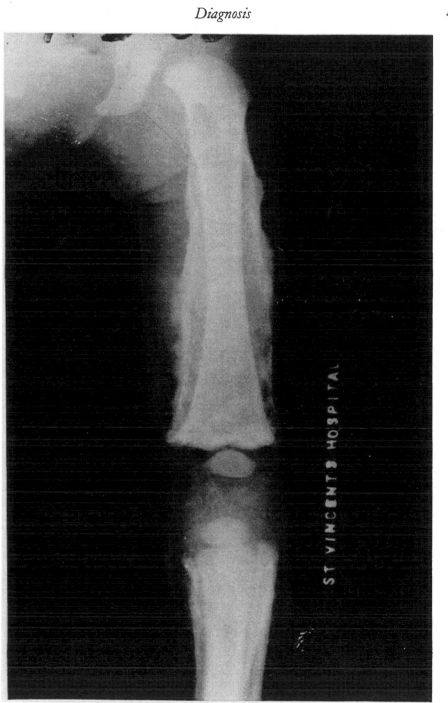

Figure 4. Female, six-and-a-half months old. Films taken four to six weeks after initial episode of inflicted trauma show extensive periosteal reaction with metaphyseal fragmentation and some calcification.

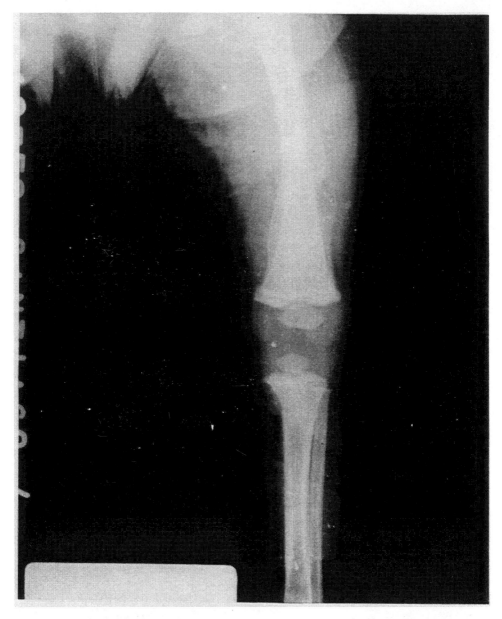

Figure 5. Female, six-and-a-half months old. Same child as in Figure 4. X-ray film taken three months later shows reparative changes, external cortical thickening, well-calcified subperiosteal reaction and squaring of the metaphysis due to new bone formation.

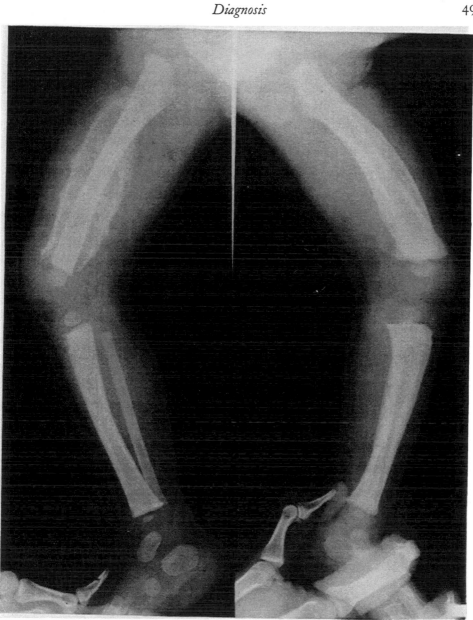

Figure 6. Male, seven months old, admitted to hospital on several occasions for "accidental" injury to thighs. The left femur shows evidence of periosteal reaction with calcification and new bone formation three to six weeks after inflicted trauma. Metaphyseal squaring also noted. The right femur in the same child shows evidence of more recently incurred injury (1–2 weeks) with subperiosteal hemorrhage, some calcification, metaphyseal fragmentation and chip fractures.

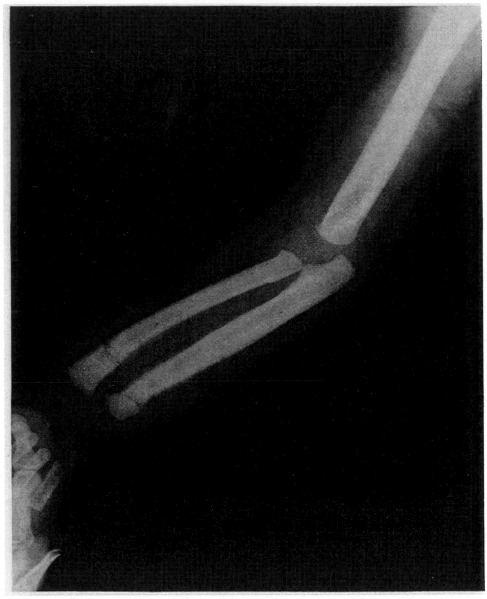

Figure 7a. Female, six-and-a-half months old, same child as in Figures 4 and 5. Inflicted injury caused x-ray evidence of fractures through distal ends of the radius and ulna.

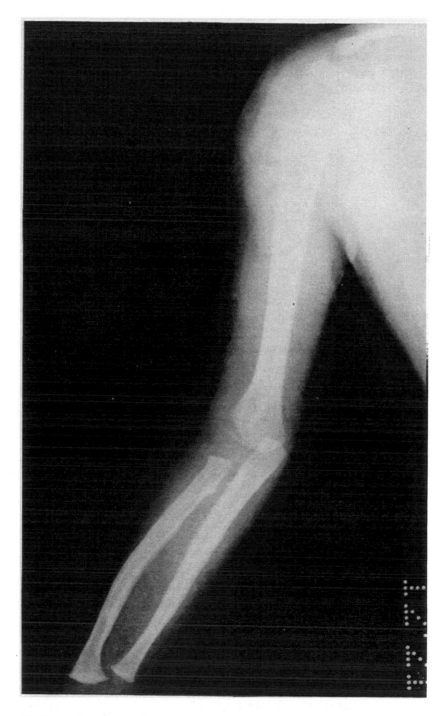

Figure 7b. X-ray taken six months after the injury indicates complete healing with no evidence of previous fractures.

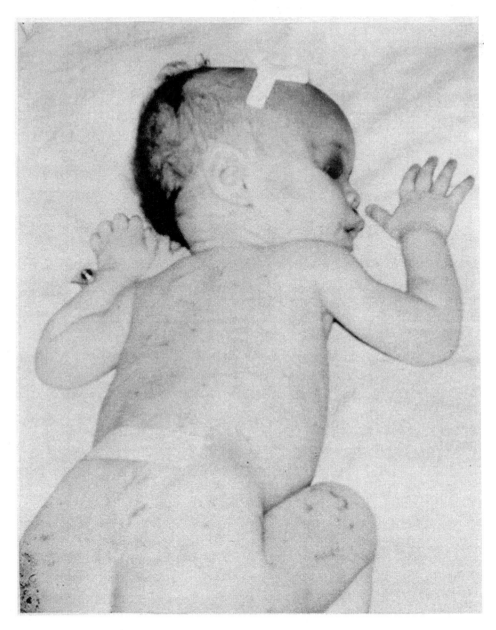

Figure 8. A 14-month-old male infant, brought to hospital emergency room by his 18-year-old mother, with a history that the child had fallen off a couch. Physical examination revealed multiple abrasions of the face, neck and body. Meningeal signs of irritation were noted on examination. Cephalohematoma was also noted. Bilateral subdural taps were positive and a spinal tap revealed evidence of meningitis. Further questioning of the mother supported suspicion of battering. Mother stated child had fever for several days, was irritable and crying continually causing parent to lose control and pummel her infant. This case exemplified maltreatment of a child involving neglect and serious abuse.

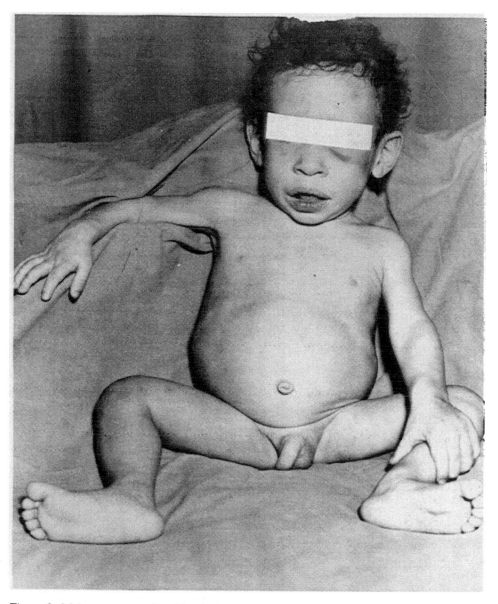

Figure 9. Male, seven months old, admitted with evidences of neglect and abuse. Child was undernourished, anemic and extremely irritable. Patient was pummeled with resultant ecchymosis around left eye and left temporal region of face. The right thigh was swollen and very tender. X-ray showed superiosteal hemorrhage and chip fractures of the right femur.

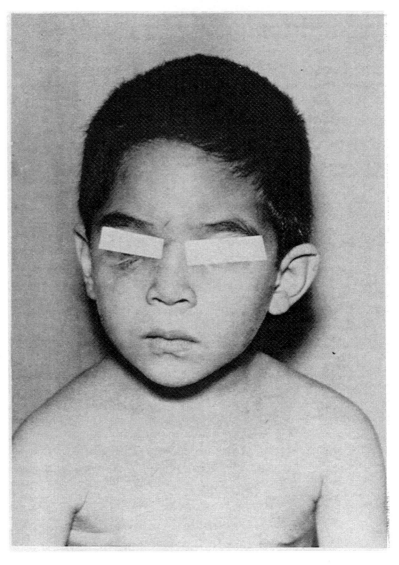

Figure 10a. Male, five years old, admitted with history of periodic beatings by parent. Physical evidence of abrasions and bruises in various stages with recent trauma to right eye and face.

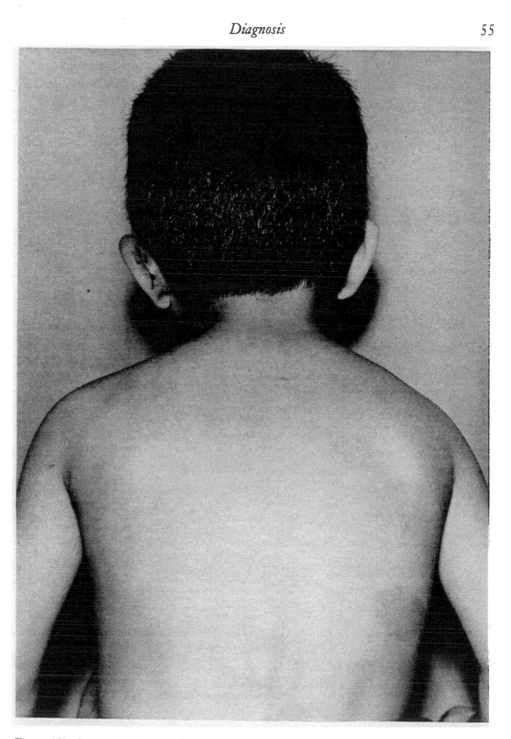

Figure 10b. Same child in posterior view showing trickling of blood behind left ear and a large associated left cephalohematoma. Scattered ecchymotic areas can also be seen on the patient's body.

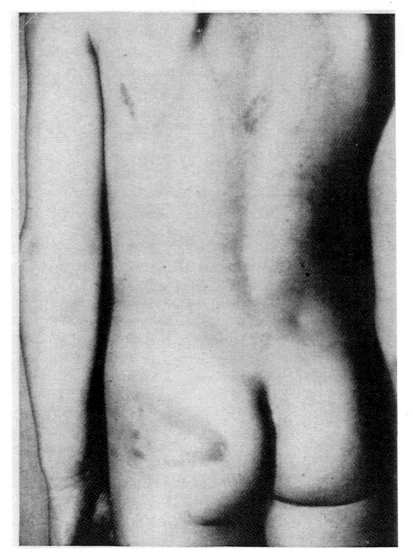

Figure 11. Male, eight-and-a-half years old. Ecchymotic areas over the body, especially on back due to inflicted injury by a sadistic parent who used belt buckles and a variety of other metal instruments.

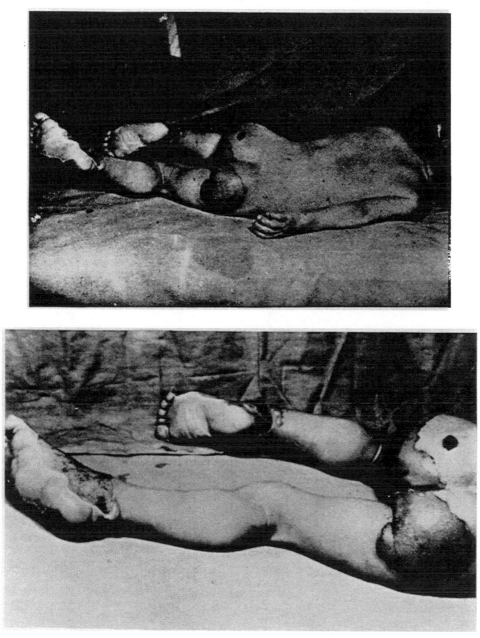

Figure 12 a, b, c. Male, three years old. Various views of burns of the buttocks, hands and feet of a child who was placed in a tub of boiling water.

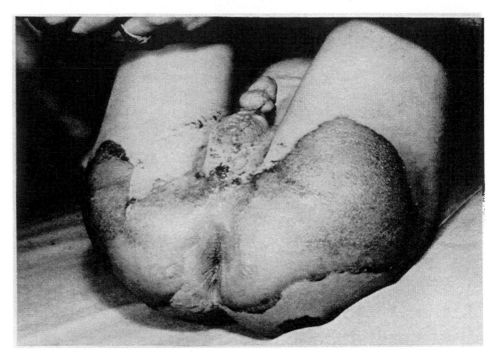

Figure 12C.

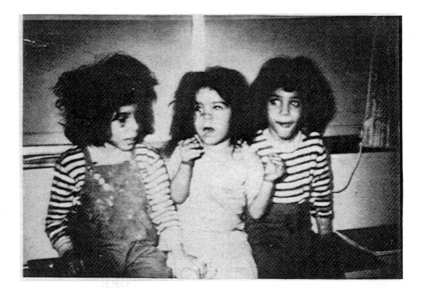

Figure 13. Three female siblings abandoned by alcoholic parents. Physical examination revealed evidences of inflicted trauma, extremely poor personal and skin hygiene with associated signs of malnutrition and anemia.

Chapter 5

SOCIAL MANIFESTATIONS

The maltreatment of children by parental abuse or neglect may occur at any age with an increased incidence in children under three years of age. In view of this, the abused infant or child cannot tell the story of how the trauma was inflicted and many young children are reluctant or afraid to tell the story.

The history that is related by the parents is very often at variance with the clinical picture and the physical findings noted on examination of the child. At times, parents are afraid to tell one another about the injury; a sitter, relative, or nurse may be reluctant to report to the parent that an accident occurred; or the baby may be injured by older siblings. Injury, often deliberately inflicted by a parent or guardian, is difficult to elicit on history.

Pertinent information can only be brought out by prolonged and adroit questioning by the physician, nurse, social worker, or hospital authority. Sometimes feelings of guilt cause the parents to withhold the true history. At times, the source of the inflicted trauma or neglect may be unknown to the person responsible for the care of the infant. Seeking-out information involves questioning any previous hospital admissions. The physician may discover that the mother has taken the child to various hospitals and doctors in an attempt to offset or negate any suspicions of parental abuse. There is usually complete denial of any knowledge of inflicted trauma to the child, and more often, the attitude of complete innocence is transmitted to the examining physician or social service authorities. Difficulty in obtaining any type of history is often encountered and a definitive diagnosis is dependent on the physical examination, x-ray findings, and the high index of suspicion on the part of the physician. There are many factors which unfavorably affect the normal infant-adult relationship leading to the maltreatment syndrome. Among the more important and more frequently reported are a history of family discord, financial stress, alcoholism, illegitimacy, poverty, perversive tendencies, drug addiction, and involvement with law enforcement agencies. Various grades of physical, mental, and social retardation are encountered in many of these abusing parents, some with obvious evidences of severe personality disorders. Environmental stresses and strains related to a life of poverty in the ghettos may serve as triggers resulting in the reported incidents of child abuse in the lower socioeconomic areas.

In recent years, there has been a dramatic rise in the number of drug-exposed babies, which may well have contributed to the escalation of abused and neglected infants. Professionals should be aware that the infant of an addicted mother is at risk of maltreatment and therefore should be protected and removed if necessary to a nonthreatening environment. The safety and welfare of the infant should be considered priority in conjunction with the referral of the parent to an appropriate drug rehabilitation program.

Many of the parents involved in the inflicted abuse and neglect of children usually are lacking in the accepted normal pattern of parental concern. They do not volunteer information to the physician, hospital authorities, social service workers, or the law enforcement agencies. The parents are usually evasive, and contradictory in their statements and are irritated by the usual routine of medical questioning. Many of these parents give no indication of any obvious guilt or remorse for their actions of inflicted abuse. It has also been noted that some do not routinely visit the child in the hospital even when he is kept for weeks or even months. These parents are not concerned and do not question the discharge date. They are not willing to follow instructions concerning future clinic visits and the medical therapy prescribed. Many show surprisingly little reaction to social service investigations or to reporting to law enforcement agencies.

The character personality of the abusing parent need not show any outside signs of neurosis or psychosis; on the contrary, they may present the disarming attitude of overprotectiveness, cooperativeness, and neatness in an attempt to mislead the physician or the social service worker. Social service workers reporting on cases encountered in our hospital have stated: "The mother's subtle lack of affect, rather compulsive neat personality, and rather socially withdrawn behavior are similar to those described in other cases where physical abuse of children in the home was later proven."

Since many of these parents do give the outward impression of devoted parents, maltreatment is often overlooked by the physician and the syndrome is not considered in the differential diagnosis. This lack of awareness by the medical profession and the postponement of social service investigations often leads to future tragedy. Time must be considered of the essence in making a diagnosis and reporting such cases of maltreatment. Serious consequences for the child involved, for the parents, and for other siblings may occur if too much time elapses between the admission of the child to the hospital and social service investigations leading to confirmation of the diagnosis. Once the diagnosis is established and reported, immediate attention must be directed toward the presence of other siblings in the family unit in order to protect them from future parental abuse.

Social service investigations have also revealed that usually one child in the family is selected and made the target for abuse and neglect, while the other siblings show evidence of overprotection. Often these abused and neglected children are made scapegoats of the parent's expression of hostility. It is also interesting to note that some of these parents seem to have perceived and experienced their own parents as unloving, cruel, and brutal. Authorities have indicated that this previous history of parental brutality has been evidenced in the parents now inflicting injury on their children expressing repressed anger and hatred. It has been stated that the battering parent of today is in many cases the battered child of yesterday.

Duncan and his associates, in 1958, studied etiological factors in first degree murder. Studies by these physicians led to the conclusion that among murderers, remorseless physical brutality at the hands of a parent had been a constant experience—brutality far beyond the ordinary excuses of discipline had been perpetrated upon them as children. It would appear that the absence of mature adult models to imitate and identify with leads to the development of the same immature behavior which may result in physical abuse to other individuals, in some cases leading to murder.

Certain childrearing practices can lead to the development of a young adult who is characterized by antisocial behavior and by pervasive difficulty in functioning within acknowledged patterns of social acceptability. When a child is exposed to repeated episodes of violence, physical abuse, verbal abuse, neglect, or rejection, the child oftentimes grows with anger and patterns his behavior on that of the model he has lived with during his childhood years.

It appears from available statistics that although the ratios of sex and race incidence did not change in the last decade, the average age of the abused victims increased significantly. Adolescents who are involved in some form of physical, sexual, as well as emotional, violence in their homes are often inclined to cover up the parental abuse because of personal guilt or shame.

As professionals, we have concentrated our efforts on the "battered baby" and the maltreated young child and failed to continue our concern for the older child over twelve years who has tolerated his abuse into adolescence. An adolescent in an already multitroubled family is confronted with personal problems of physical and sexual development as well as a lack of parental communication. Behavioral problems of an adolescent in a disrupted family unit cause the parental stressful situations that lead to adolescent abuse. In instances of adolescent abuse, there is a misalignment between a youth's "growing up" and parent's "change of life," leaving both the parents and youth vulnerable to interfamilial conflict and violence. The maltreatment syndrome of children should therefore also encompass the teenager who is being increasingly recognized and reported as a victim of abuse, particularly in the areas of sexual exploitation. Many abused adolescents tend to escape from their maltreatment by leaving the family unit only to find societal abuse and neglect being inflicted upon them as "runaways" and the "throwaway" children of our society.

There has been a lack of medical and social services available to the abused and neglected teenage with resultant increases in the incidence of juvenile suicides, teenage pregnancies, delinquency, drug addiction, alcoholism, and adolescent sexual exploitation and pornography. The development of services responsive to the needs of maltreated adolescents should be available to professionals treating adolescents in the community.

In evaluating cases of child abuse and neglect at the New York Foundling Hospital Center for Parent and Child Development, it was found that the maltreated child is usually the victim of emotionally crippled parents who have had unfortunate circumstances surrounding their own childhood. The abusive parent appears to react to his own child as a result of past personal experiences of loneliness, lack of protection and love. Some of these parents have been raised by a variety of foster parents during their own childhood. The parents are unable to react normally to the needs of their own children. He or she is usually immature, narcissistic, demanding, impulsive, depressed, and aggressive.

He or she tends to be a social isolate of minimal self-esteem, lacking a parental role model, looking to the child to provide warmth and attention not forthcoming from his or her own parents. They appear unwilling to accept responsibility as a parent. It seems they have distorted perception of a particular child at a particular stage in its development. When the child is not able to perform, according to expectations, the parent may be triggered into a reaction leading to inflicted abuse.

Divorce, alcoholism, drug addiction, mental retardation, recurring mental illness, unemployment, and financial stress are important factors often present in the family structure of abusing parents. These stress factors all play major roles in leading the potentially abusive parent to strike out at a particular child during a crisis situation. The three components, namely, a potentially abusing parent, a "special" child who may be hyperactive, handicapped, or "different"; and a sudden crisis are the necessary ingredients that give rise to child abuse and battering.

The possibility of abuse or neglect should be considered when several of the following factors are present:

The child seems unduly afraid of his parents.

The child is unusually fearful generally.

The child is kept confined, as in a crib or playpen (or cage), for overlong periods of time.

The child shows evidence of repeated skin or other injuries.

The child's injuries are inappropriately treated in terms of bandages and medication.

The child appears to be undernourished.

The child is given inappropriate food, drink, or medicine.

The child is dressed inappropriately for weather conditions.

The child shows evidence of overall poor care.

The child cries often.

The child is described as "different" or "bad" by the parents.

The child does indeed seem "different" in physical or emotional makeup.

The child takes over the role of parent and tries to be protective and takes care of the parent's needs.

The child is notably destructive and aggressive.

The child is notably passive and withdrawn.

The parent or parents discourage social contact.

The parent seems to be very much alone and to have no one to call upon when the stresses of parenthood get to be overwhelming.

The parent is unable to open up and share problems with an interested listener and appears to trust nobody.

The parent makes no attempt to explain the child's most obvious injuries or offers absurd, contradictory explanations for the injuries.

The parent seems to be quite detached from the child's problems.

The parent reveals inappropriate awareness of the seriousness of the child's condition and concentrates on complaining about irrelevant problems unrelated to the injured/neglected appearance of the child.

The parent blames a sibling or third party for the child's injury.

The parent shows signs of lack of control or fear of losing control.

The parent delays in taking the child in for medical care, either in case of injury or illness, or for routine checkups.

The parent appears to be misusing drugs or alcohol.

The parent ignores the child's crying or reacts with extreme impatience.

The parent has unrealistic expectations of the child: that he should be mature beyond his years; that he or she should "mother" the parent (role reversal).

The parent indicates in the course of the conversation that he/she was reared in a motherless, unloving atmosphere; that he or she was neglected or abused as a child; that he or she grew up under conditions of harsh discipline and feels that it is right to impose those same conditions on his or her own children.

The parent appears to be of borderline intelligence, psychotic, or psychopathic. (Most laypersons will find it difficult to make a judgment here. It might be better for the observer to note whether the parent exhibits the minimal intellectual equipment to bring up a child; whether the parent is generally rational or irrational in manner; whether the parent is cruel, sadistic, and lacking remorse for hurtful actions.)

In summary, some of the characteristics of abusive parents include impulsivity, dependency, age inappropriateness, sadomasochism, egocentricity, and narcissism. Abusive parents are immature, demanding, isolated, depressed, angry, nontrusting, lacking self-esteem and self-control. However, it must be remembered that the psychodynamics of child abuse involve two victims—the parent and the child. To help the child, we have to connect with the parents and recognize their suffering without condoning their actions. If we are not understanding and compassionate with them, we are likely to lose them and the children.

Chapter 6

PREVENTIVE MEASURES

MEDICAL RESPONSIBILITIES

The incidence of the maltreatment syndrome in children is increasing. It is obviously a problem of national importance calling for the full cooperative resources and efforts of the medical, social, and legal organizations of this country.

Various reports from child protective agencies reveal that some physicians are still unwilling to accept the fact that parents can and often do willfully inflict serious damage to their children or even kill them. Stimulated by the increasing reports of this pediatric problem of serious import, the educational process of bringing this syndrome to the attention of the medical student, the hospital trainee, and the practicing physician has progressed. Media and literary information on child abuse has challenged the reluctance of primary care physicians to recognize and interpret parental dysfunction as a possible cause of inflicted trauma in children. Multiple fractures in various stages of resolution, dislocations, subdural hematomas, purpuric lesions of the skin, severe burns, unexplained malnutrition, and failure to thrive should all be reasons for suspect by the alert physician.

Society is seeing evidence of parents who strike out against their children being reported in every day newspaper accounts, television, and movies. The medical profession is now faced with a greater responsibility of early intervention and protection of the maltreated child who comes to their attention. The moral responsibility of the examining physician is to the maltreated child; he must be cognizant of the fact that over 50 percent of these abused children are liable to secondary injuries or death if appropriate steps are not taken to rescue them from their life-threatening environment.

The physician in practice should refer suspected cases involving maltreatment in children to the hospital for thorough diagnostic medical study and social investigations. The hospital remains the proper place for initial diagnosis and treatment of suspected child abuse and neglect. Accurate diagnosis and disposition are facilitated efficiently and quickly. Monitoring of parent-child interactions by nursing, social service, and other staff can also be accomplished. It also provides a safe haven for the child during the diagnostic work-up. If hospitalization of the child is not practical, the physician should report the case to the child protective agency in the community or to law enforcement, who in turn will take appropriate legal action to protect the child. If the physician is a house officer on duty in a hospital facility and suspects child abuse, the child should be admitted overnight for social service consultation, whether or not the severity of the injury warrants it. This will give the physician the opportunity to ask the hospital social worker to interview the parents. The house officer and social worker can then report their findings to the child abuse hospital team which decides whether or not to report the case to the child protective agency. The final diagnosis of child abuse should involve the expert knowledge of a multidisciplinary team of medical professionals and social workers. The roles of the members of a multidisciplinary team need to be carefully defined so that members of the team know what to expect of their colleagues.

Whenever necessary, the physician must testify as an expert witness, interpreting his medical findings and answering questions relating to the specific inflicted abuse and injury. He or she must be prepared to make a specific diagnosis and case management recommendations which will result in protecting the child and treating the abusive parent. Treatment of the child's injuries must be followed by the immediate reporting of the abuse or neglect to the appropriate agencies who are responsible for the investigation and assessment of the child's home and family situation.

The medical societies have reappraised their approach to this difficult problem and have disseminated information to their membership concerning the early intervention and management of child maltreatment. This problem of parental dysfunction resulting in child abuse has become a topic of top priority discussed at state, regional, and national medical meetings. The doctors' increased interest and recognition of the maltreatment syndrome in children should lead to more primary and secondary preventive measures that will hopefully decrease the future incidence of child abuse, neglect, injury, and death.

Every physician who has under his charge or care any child suspected of having wounds, fractures, dislocations, or burns due to suspected inflicted injury, should take colored photographs of the injuries. The above can be adequately documented with the use of a simple instant camera, a self-developing camera, or a 35mm close-up system. At least two photographs should be taken of each finding, one including identifying landmarks and one close-up of the lesions. All photos must be identified by child's name, age, date of birth, date photograph was taken, location of injury, and name of the photographer. Photographs of the child after admission to the hospital will greatly assist in confirming and documenting lesions and body damage due to abuse when they are presented to the law enforcement agencies and the courts. Physicians are usually permitted to explain and illustrate their testimony with a photograph. Difficulties usually arise during court procedures when the abused child is presented in perfect health after a period of hospitalization and convalescence without photographic evidences of inflicted abuse. The court in such cases may find it difficult to justify removal of the child from the mother under the presenting circumstances of the child's physical well-being and holding to the concept of "mother belongs to child" and "child belongs to mother."

The following index of suspicion may be helpful to the physician before reporting cases of maltreatment:

History

1. Characteristic age—usually under three years.
2. General health of child—indicative of neglect.
3. Characteristic distribution of fractures.
4. Disproportionate amounts of soft tissue injury.
5. Evidence that injuries occurred at different times, with lesions in various stages of resolution.
6. Cause of recent trauma not known.
7. Previous history of similar episodes and multiple visits to various hospitals.
8. Date of injury prior to admission to hospital—delay in seeking medical help.
9. Child brought to hospital for complaint other than one associated with abuse and/or neglect, e.g., cold, headache, stomachaches, etc.
10. Reluctance of parents or caretakers to give information.
11. History related by parents or caretaker is usually at complete variance with the clinical picture and the physical findings noted on examinations of the child.

12. Parents' inappropriate reaction to severity of injury.
13. Family discord or financial stress, alcoholism, psychosis, drug addiction and inconsistent social history that varies according to intake worker.

Physical Examination

1. Signs of general neglect, failure to thrive, poor skin hygiene, malnutrition, withdrawal, irritability, repressed personality.
2. Bruises, abrasions, burns, soft tissue swellings, bites, hematomas, ocular damage, old healed lesions.
3. Evidences of dislocation and/or fractures of the extremities.
4. Unexplained symptoms of an acute abdomen—ruptured viscera.
5. Neurologic findings associated with brain damage.
6. Coma, convulsions, death.
7. Symptoms of drug withdrawal or drug intoxication.

Differential Diagnosis

1. Scurvy and rickets.
2. Infantile cortical hyperostosis.
3. Syphilis of infancy.
4. Osteogenesis imperfecta.
5. Neurologic, organic brain damage.
6. Accidental trauma.

Radiologic Manifestations

1. Subperiosteal hemorrhages.
2. Epiphyseal separations.
3. Periosteal shearing.
4. Metaphyseal fragmentation.
5. Previously healed periosteal calcifications.
6. "Squaring" of the metaphysis.

After the physician has decided to report a case of child abuse, he should explain to the parents the reason for filing a report as mandated by the State Child Abuse Law. It should be made clear that these findings of suspected abuse of the child are being reported to the child protective agency in an effort to protect the child from further injury. In reporting the medical findings, the physician should be cautious and make definite efforts not to accuse any individual of the inflicted trauma until all the evidence is at hand. Parents may be suspected but should never be accused. Parents should be made aware of the situation and

offered assistance in resolving the problems within the family that may
have led to the maltreatment. The physician may, with justification, be
angered by the battering parents, but withholding such hostility will
contribute to the future protection of the child and other siblings. An
empathetic, concerned, nonjudgmental, objective physician dealing with
the maltreated child can affect the beginning of change in the parent-
child relationship.

The physician should inform the parents that under the requirements
of the law, a formal report must be filed of any injury to a child that is
not clearly explained. Making such a report to the child protective
agency is a means of securing the help and supportive family services
needed in solving some of the parental problems. When properly
approached, many parents will be more trusting and will sense a feeling
of relief that possible assistance and intervention is forthcoming. The
reporting process should be aimed at helping the multitroubled family,
not at intensifying an already existing explosive family situation. Developing a good initial relationship with the family is crucial to the creation
of an effective long-term treatment plan.

The physician's first responsibility is to the child, encouraging immediate removal of the child from a life-threatening environment if necessary.
Once the child has been treated and protected from further abuse, the
physician and social worker can then turn their attention to the parents
or caretakers. In most instances, the child protective agencies will assume
responsibility for the complete evaluation and disposition of the child to
its own home under supervision, to the courts, to a child-caring institution,
or to a foster home. It cannot be overemphasized that the problem
demands the most delicate handling by all involved disciplines. The
physician's intervention is important if the child is to be protected from
further abuse. The physician who is reluctant to report or does not want
to become involved in cases of suspected child abuse and battering, aids
and abets those guilty of maltreating children. The American physician
can no longer legally remain silent under presently existing mandatory
reporting laws in all of the states and the District of Columbia.

A physician's responsibilities in the problem of child abuse can be
encouraged and supported by the existence of a hospital child abuse
committee. This type of child abuse team officially designated by hospital authorities, would review all child abuse cases and make specific
recommendations as to the social, medical, and legal measures needed
for the protection of the maltreated child. A committee of this type

should have a multidisciplinary team, including a physician as chairman, a social worker, nurse, a hospital administrator, and a mental health specialist. The committee would coordinate in-service education programs relating to child maltreatment for members of the hospital staff, for patients, and for the community at large. The committee also assumes responsibility for collecting and analyzing statistics on child abuse emergency room visits, reporting, and follow-up. The team approach capitalizes on the collective observations and opinions of its diverse membership.

Kempe has proposed the development of regional metropolitan centers for the study and care of abused and neglected children. Within these centers, experienced professionals would evaluate methods of early case finding, develop means to identify the family that can be strengthened, coordinate community services, and protect children from physical abuse. In addition, a center of this type could evaluate current methods of care of the abused child and his parents and provide the impetus for new therapeutic approaches.

Hospital-sponsored seminars on child abuse can provide interns and residents in all departments with information necessary to implement child abuse laws. Educational programs sponsored by the medical societies will orient practicing physicians to the problem and also disseminate information to the medical, social, and legal disciplines involved with child abuse.

The law is definite as to who should report, stating "any physician, surgeon, dentist, osteopath, optometrist, chiropractor, podiatrist, resident, intern, registered nurse, or Christian Science practitioner having reasonable cause to suspect that a child is an abused or neglected child shall report or cause reports to be made." The concept of broadening the class of persons required to report beyond physicians has gained considerable support in recent years. The structure of our presently existing child abuse laws imposes a high degree of responsibility for generating reports on the physician, nurse, teacher, and social worker alike.

The physician must bear in mind that he need have only reasonable cause to suspect. He need make no definitive diagnosis and is not required to make any accusation as to who caused the suspected injuries. It is important to note here that the law specifically protects the reporting person against any civil or criminal proceedings resulting from such reporting when made in good faith.

In Summary, The physician's responsibility in suspected cases of child abuse and neglect should include the following steps:

1. Making the diagnosis of the maltreatment syndrome.
2. Immediate intervention and admission of the child to the hospital if necessary.
3. Complete assessment and treatment—medical history, physical examination, skeletal survey, colored photographs of injuries.
4. Report case to the appropriate community Department of Social Service or Child Protective Unit responsible for investigation.
5. During hospitalization of child, request necessary medical consultations and social worker investigation.
6. Conference within seventy-two hours with members of the Hospital's Child Abuse Committee.
7. Arrange referral to program of care for child and parent with multidisciplinary staff.

SOCIAL RESPONSIBILITIES

Child Protective Agencies and Social Service

In 1958, the United Nations Declaration of the Rights of Children set forth the following goal: "Whereas mankind owes to the child the best it has to give ... the child shall be protected against all forms of neglect, cruelty and exploitation." The fact that we have fallen short of achieving that goal is painfully clear from our national statistics on child maltreatment. Despite governmental support, the problem continues its devastation of children and families at risk. Ironically, increased awareness has led to a dramatic increase in the number of suspected abuse and neglect cases being reported to child protection services, thus adding to the strain on a system that is already overloaded. Child protection workers are often confronted with a large backlog of pending cases. Many workers report difficulties in obtaining long-term community human support services, especially housing, for the families under their care. Anxious and overworked, they are often plagued by feelings of helplessness.

Laws that mandate the reporting of suspected child abuse cannot, by themselves, protect child victims. It is what happens after the report is made that is important in preventing further abuse. The evaluation of a child abuse report requires extensive time, energy, and skill on the part of many different professionals—social workers, teachers, police, judges, psychologists, psychiatrists, nurses, lawyers, and physicians. An inaccurate, incomplete, or hurried investigation can lead to a faulty conclusion, with far-reaching and devastating effects on the maltreated child.

More active casework techniques must be established which will reach out toward the neglecting parents and abused children. Only through a comprehensive social service approach can the evidence that is presented by the medical profession be effectively utilized in bringing about the rehabilitation of these parents from a grossly inadequate situation into a more responsible parenting role.

Social service agencies throughout the country play a very important part in helping the countless number of disturbed parents who strike out against society through their abnormal behavior of aggression toward the child. These social agencies must be able to recognize and be prepared to treat family problems which feed into child maltreatment. They must be prepared to alleviate or eliminate the conditions and factors in the environment that can lead to parental delinquency.

In performing a proper assessment, the caseworker or investigator should talk privately with each member of the child's family. Such interviews can reveal the nature of family interactions, attitudes of family members toward each other, and the child's role within the family. Teachers, neighbors, and friends can also provide vital information concerning obvious changes in the child's appearance, behavior, and personality. All of this takes a great deal of time and energy, but it is necessary if the information required to bring a court action is to be obtained. Unfortunately, some agencies lack the staff and resources to conduct such a complete and thorough investigation.

The increase in the number of child abuse complaints, the scarcity of foster homes for children who have been removed from abusive environments, and the difficulty of obtaining human support services (especially housing) for troubled families all have contributed to the child protection system's problems.

The Children's Division of the American Humane Association undertook a survey to assess and evaluate the effectiveness of child protective services across the nation. Among other facts, it was noted that there was a growing awareness that in too many communities too little was being done toward family-centered casework service dealing with the protection of children. There seemed to be a lack of trained social workers in the field of child protection. Many of the child protective agencies were understaffed and overloaded with child maltreatment reports resulting in a large number of abused children falling through the cracks of an inadequate, poorly functioning child protective system. There was also a lack of child protective agencies in certain communities.

Child protection was first highlighted by the public protest and concern over the treatment of Mary Ellen, a child who was maltreated in New York City in 1874, by the removal of the abused child and punishment of the offending parents. With the passing of time, child advocates have emphasized a more compassionate and understanding approach encouraging a reaching out effort to help abusive parents before the need for punishment.

The Children's Division of the American Humane Association has often emphasized that: "In many sections of the country excellent planning makes provision for a wide range of welfare services and activities in a voluntary board management and control, or in the public auspices such as county, state or federal government. These make available to the community the family patterns of health services, family counseling, child welfare services, recreation facilities and public assistance. More specifically they provide financial assistance to families; financial and other aid to mothers and children; clinical aid with respect to health problems; psychological and psychiatric consultation and treatment; advice on family problems and marital difficulties; day care for children, foster home care, adoptions and institutional services." They also have stated, rightfully and most emphatically, that these services are open to anyone who needs them and asks for them. Unfortunately, most parents who neglect their children do not ask for these services. It is therefore the responsibility of child care and child protective agencies in the community to provide human support services to these potentially abusive parents through case findings and investigation.

Communities must develop within their bureaucracies a multidisciplinary approach to dealing with cases of child maltreatment. There must be a mechanism whereby professionals from different agencies can exchange information on detection, prevention, investigation, and treatment. This would allow child protection workers, lawyers, physicians, nurses, judges, law enforcement officials, and educators to draw on each other's expertise. During coordinated discussions, professionals who previously had little or no contact with each other could gain important information. They could develop a mutual respect for and understanding of each other's responsibilities and could close dangerous gaps in their communication.

A multidisciplinary approach of this type should include a case review process using a comprehensive standardized form and computerized data storage and retrieval base so that all pertinent information would be available in one location. This would minimize the chances of error, prevent duplication of effort, and allow cases to be tracked for evaluation purposes.

The New York State Youth Commission, several years ago, in attempting to define the rights of all children, stated in clear terms what they have called:

THE CHILDREN'S BILL OF RIGHTS

For each child, regardless of race, color or creed:
1. The right to the affection and intelligent guidance of understanding parents.
2. The right to be raised in a decent home in which he or she is adequately fed, clothed, and sheltered.
3. The rights to the benefits of religious guidance and training.
4. The right to a school program which in addition to sound academic training offers maximum opportunity for individual development and preparation for living.
5. The right to receive constructive discipline for the proper development of good character, conduct and habits.
6. The right to be secure in his or her community against all influence detrimental to proper and wholesome development.
7. The right to individual selection of free and wholesome recreation.
8. The right to live in a community in which adults practice the belief that the welfare of their children is of primary importance.
9. The right to receive good adult example.
10. The right to a job commensurate with his or her ability, training and experience, and protection against physical or moral employment hazards which adversely affect wholesome development.
11. The right to early diagnosis and treatment of physical handicap and mental and social maladjustments at public expense whenever necessary.

This bill of rights not only enumerates the rights of children, but also indicates the obligations and the responsibilities of society and of all parents. It is in the best interests of the child that should motivate the social service worker in rendering the best possible case investigation and assessment. The neglected and abused child becomes a ward of the social service worker or child protective agency under this bill of rights, until the threatening factors in the child's environment are removed.

It is the responsibility of the social service worker to foster through contact, investigation, and understanding the rights of children and the duties and obligations of parents to their children. It is through the recognition of these mutual rights that family relationships become healthier. This in turn results in the removal of factors responsible for the inflicted neglect and abuse of children found in present-day society.

To punish the juvenile has not been the answer to the problem of delinquency, nor does punishing parents who have neglected or abused their children bring any real help to the parents or the children at risk. The abusing parent or caretaker inflicting trauma on a helpless child must be assisted sociologically, psychiatrically, and medically to break the cycle of violence breeding violence from generation to generation. The personality disorders which are found in many of these abusive parents, including immaturity, depression, violence, inadequate parenting, mental deficiency, and other physical, emotional, and moral inadequacies must be defined and treated to eliminate any aspect of parental dysfunction. These victims of modern frustrations and antisocial living, triggered by economic and environmental, moral and emotional tensions, need help. For example, one source of help may be to provide the parent at home with a homemaker. This individual can serve as a lay therapist, can serve as a maternal figure to "mother" the mother, and can assist the immature mother in childrearing and housekeeping practices. Child care, parenting education, housing, job training, and drug rehabilitation are some of the other human support programs that can be made available to the troubled parent.

The community must face up to the responsibility that the maltreatment of children is a problem of increasing incidence and importance. The communities throughout the country must establish and maintain services which will protect the child and rehabilitate the parents when physical, financial, and emotional problems make them unable to cope with the stresses and strains of everyday living. Government cannot afford to further neglect this all-important problem involving the parents of today and the future parents of tomorrow. The physical, moral, spiritual, and emotional status of America's future generation depends on society's reaction toward this problem of maltreatment today.

A maltreated child is, and must be, the concern and responsibility of schools, hospitals, voluntary child care agencies, law enforcement, family courts, drug rehabilitation programs, and mental health facilities. These facilities must coordinate their activities and communicate any information on child abuse to the community child protective agency. The effectiveness of any child protective agency is dependent on its coordination, cooperation, and communication with the social, medical, and legal professionals on all aspects of the maltreatment syndrome of children.

In the publication "Community Cooperation for Better Child Protection" by Vincent DeFrancis, child protection is defined as:

> A specialized case work service on behalf of children who are neglected, abused, exploited or cruelly treated. It recognizes that neglect usually results where parents, unable to function adequately because of inability to cope with their own problems, fail to meet the basic physical, medical or emotional needs of their children. The focus of the service is preventive and impunitive and is geared toward a rehabilitation of the home and a treatment of the motivating factors which underlie the neglect. This implies that parents and children are given help with those problems which have directly affected the parents' ability to provide proper care and service. The service is usually initiated on a complaint or referral from sources outside the family. The agency providing protective services has authority granted it by law or a charter which imposes an obligation to provide the service when needed and which grants the right to explore and study and evaluate the facts of neglect and their effect on children. The agency has responsibility for invoking the authority of the juvenile court with such action as is necessary to secure adequate protection, care and treatment of children whose parents are unable or unwilling to use the help offered by the agency.

The child protective agencies can meet their obligations and responsibilities only if they receive the community's cooperation which it is organized to serve. The community must give personal and financial assistance to the child protective agencies. Without the full cooperation of city, county, and state child care organizations, child protective agencies cannot effectively function and fulfill their responsibilities in protecting at-risk children.

Child protective programs must be organized where they are not available. Appropriate administrative structures with authority must be supported through adequate financial budgets. Community resources are the fuel with which the child protective agencies operate. Every member of society can truly protect and prevent a child from being a victim of abuse and neglect by providing necessary support to the child protective programs in the community. The effectiveness of any child protective agency and the results that it produces runs parallel with the support it receives from the concerned members of the community.

The 1993 Executive Summary of the U. S. Advisory Board on Child Abuse and Neglect includes:

> ... we as a nation must overcome the isolation and tensions created by the demands of modern life. We must create caring communities which support

families that shelter and nurture children. We must take the time to see the need and to lend a hand. Above all, we must put the interests of children first and take steps that will allow them to grow, achieve their potential and become contributing members of society. A proper child maltreatment strategy will not only protect children from harm. It will help them thrive.

PREVENTION OF CHILD ABUSE

The community and the child care agencies have several responsibilities in the field of child maltreatment, namely, the identification and diagnosis of child maltreatment; the provision of therapeutic multidisciplinary human support services and an educational program that will allow professionals and paraprofessionals to fulfill their responsibilities in the identification, diagnosis, and treatment of child abuse. Primary prevention is also an important responsibility of the community. In this area, the social, medical, and legal disciplines must offer their resources and work collectively in order to more effectively control the rising incidence of child abuse. To achieve any success in the area of prevention, massive programs on parenting and family care must be developed and implemented. Other efforts that can provide effective preventive services include:

1. The establishment of "parent helplines," "hot lines," or "lifelines" such as the organization called CALM (Child Abuse Listening Mediation), started in 1970. The CALM hot line functions as a crisis intervention service which provides the distressed, potentially abusive parent with an immediate outlet with someone to talk to. This type of crisis intervention can oftentimes prevent a parent from striking out at a child during a time of crisis. This service to the parent also provides a means of identifying parents in need of help so that referrals can be made to appropriate community family services. In many areas of the country, these crisis intervention hot lines are manned by volunteers who are able to provide information of immediate help to the caller.

2. Volunteers have in the past provided a source of important contributions in the field of child welfare. In the last two decades, they have become involved and supplemented service staffs of child abuse prevention and treatment efforts. In this area, they have proven to be effective in direct services to clients ranging from answering "hot lines" to working directly with abusive parents as

lay therapists. A variety of volunteer responsibilities in child abuse and neglect programs have been developed in recent years and have been used successfully in the interdisciplinary approach to intervention and therapy.

Trained volunteers are important assets in any program dealing with abusive parents and their children. The basic requirements for paraprofessional volunteerism include a maturity developed through having lived and survived difficult life experiences, emotional stability, nonjudgmental warmth, empathy, patience, honesty, and a basic capacity of caring and a willingness to give time and concern in helping others.

Volunteers have proven their effectiveness in a variety of programs including: Parent aides (SCAN); crisis hot lines (Parental Stress Services); self-help groups (Parents Anonymous); surrogate parents; lay therapists (shelter treatment homes and outpatient programs); day care centers; therapeutic nurseries; and crisis family centers. In addition, they have provided leadership roles in child advocacy groups (Citizens' Committees and Task Forces); medical and legal services to families; education and public awareness campaigns; fund raising for child abuse treatment; and prevention programs.

3. Teach parenting within the school system. Establish a curriculum that will allow young people in elementary and high schools to learn the awesome responsibilities of parenting. Courses in child abuse and family violence should be included to allow students who have been abused to recognize their potential for violence and thereby seek preventive professional help. Providing educational parenting experiences to young people will help to reestablish the stability of the family unit. It's never too early to learn parenting.

Schools need massive doses of outside help to mobilize the personal resources of teachers, parents, and children. Such help is often at hand in the form of a variety of nonprofit programs that can function in any community. One such is EPIC— Effective Parenting Information for Children—an organization based in the State University College at Buffalo, New York.

EPIC, funded by state agencies, county youth boards and vate foundations, is a sort of package program that can be brought into any school or school district whose educators and community leaders want to support it. Parent participation is fundamental. EPIC's philosophy is rooted in the proposition that destructive juvenile behavior and adult maltreatment of children are both primarily due to lack of effective—or any—parenting education. Thus, one component of its program prepares children of all ages to be responsible adults with positive parenting skills. Another gives workshops in parenting for parents of children in two different age groups. Parents of young children come to grips with such topics as fostering self-esteem, single parenting, communicating with teachers, and coping with daily conflicts and family crises; parents of adolescents tackle such issues as teenage values, adolescent suicide, identity and independence, emerging sexuality, and teen pregnancy. Parent effectiveness training programs such as P.E.T. provide adult education in the skills of parenting. The P.E.T. program was established by Dr. Thomas Gordon and has been found effective in this area of providing parents with child rearing information. The need to provide parents with this information is important in developing good parent-child relationships. These healthy experiences and expressions of good parenting can prevent some of the traumatic crisis situations which trigger child abuse in the family unit.

Another major area of prevention lies in sex education beyond the physical-sexual level—a human sexuality curriculum that includes and emphasizes the understanding of family life skills, and the long-term effects and responsibilities of childrearing.

Teenagers must be made aware that having sex is filled with emotional, physical, and social consequences. Sex education in the schools should therefore include such things as family values, a healthy acceptance of the responsibilities that go with sexuality, emotional stability in marital relationships, and willingness to to accept the consequences of one's actions. This kind of comprehensive education in human sexuality can meet the real real developmental needs of teenagers searching for their sexual identity and the responsibilities that go with becoming a parent. Lest we forget the other parent, namely the father, let us remember that parenthood is a mutual responsibility and so all efforts must be made to provide supportive services to the teenage father as well. Increasingly more involvement of the father is being mandated by law.

4. The concept of a "health visitor" to act as a primary health screener for entire families is another positive effort in primary prevention. The health visitor as proposed by Dr. C. Henry Kempe would provide an assessment of the parent-child relationships; advise on common well-child problems; provide a liaison with available health community resources; and screen for childhood developmental abnormalities. The health visitor would initiate regular visits with the young mother soon after her discharge with her baby from the hospital. This intervention would provide primary preventive measures to a parent in a nonthreatening manner and establish a strong link between the private and public health care system of our communities. This type of early intervention as proposed by Dr. Kempe would substantially add to the hopes of reducing the incidence of child maltreatment. A good plan would be one that would have periodic visitation to families by professionals or paraprofessionals that would offer help before the occurrence of a crisis situation. This is about the best type of preventive pediatrics available today. Implementation of a friendly visitor program within communities can serve as an important and effective therapeutic modality. Parent aides and homemakers can help parents who are in stressful situations and prevent them from becoming involved in crisis situations leading to neglect and abuse.

All of these home health care services emphasize prevention designed to having children remain at home with their natural parents. The nurse, social worker, or paraprofessional visiting the home provides an early periodic screening program for the detection of child maltreatment. This helper should be able to give direct services within her or his own competency and be able to prescribe and obtain needed services such as homemakers, home health aides, and the variety of human support and respite services for the parents and child that may be required. They should also be qualified to provide on-going practical information as well as counseling to the parents on all aspects of childrearing, child nutrition, and effective parenting. Training of these professional and paraprofessional "family helpers" in the broad provision of these home health services is an essential first step in this preventive approach. The priorities for recipients of these preventive services should focus on parents, especially single parents with preschool or school-age children living at home.

5. Day Care Centers, Family Day Care Centers, Infant Day Care Centers and Crisis Nurseries may well be a means of providing families and children with the necessary human resources necessary to maintain family stability and, in many cases, prevent child abuse. These child care programs allow parents to obtain needed relief from the constant presence and pressures of children that can cause or trigger child abuse. Day Care programs can provide an educational experience for the child and a therapeutic respite for parents.

6. Mother-Child programs that provide support systems to the young mother in the development of a parent-child relationship. A model mother-child program developed at the New York Foundling Hospital in 1972 provides a residential setting and a variety of services enabling young mothers to grow into parents who can accept responsibility for themselves and their children. The program assists the young mother who wishes to keep her baby by providing her with a homelike atmosphere in a residence of the Foundling Hospital while being assisted in the development of parenting skills. During her stay in the residence, the mother is also given the opportunity to complete her education or receive some type of on-the-job training in an area which will assist her in developing skills that will help her secure future employment. The mother and child remain in the program from one year to eighteen months.

7. Screening for the high-risk mothers during prenatal and postpartum periods offers a unique opportunity for preventive child maltreatment intervention. Immediate involvement with the parent by attending physicians, nurses, social workers, and health visitors will help avoid the parental misbehavior that leads to child neglect, failure to thrive, and physical injury to the child.
Although we are more aware of the psychodynamics of child abuse today, we are not as cognizant of the predictive parameters of the problem. It is obvious that if one could develop a predictive scale of potential child abusers and/or abnormal parenting experiences and practices, early effective interven-

tion could be facilitated and thereby prevent damage to the victim, namely the newborn infant or child.

Drs. C. Henry Kempe and Jane Gray have recognized the importance of early detection during the prenatal and neonatal periods. These periods offer the observer an excellent opportunity to study the parents' attitudes, personality structure, social contacts, degree of intrafamilial communication, their values and their "hang ups." It also provides during the neonatal period an opportunity to asses the newborn infant's behavior, as well as parent-child interactions, parent-parent relationships and any indicator of potentially harmful child rearing patterns. Intervention during these critical sensitive and emotionally laden periods can prevent parent-induced damage to the child and allow providing the human network of support for the parents that will insure the child's fullest physical, emotional, and intellectual potential for development.

Gray, Kempe, and coworkers, utilizing an interview, a questionnaire and labor, delivery and postpartum observations, have established that perinatal assessment and simple intervention with mothers at "high risk for abnormal parenting practices" significantly improves the infants' chances for escaping future physical injury. Some "high-risk" characteristics include a history of child abuse, adolescent pregnancy, financial problems, social isolation, alcoholism, drug addiction, and inadequate child care arrangements.

Our concern for children must begin with the mother's pregnancy, her feelings about the pregnancy, and her anxiety and fears during the prenatal period. This type of attention to the mother's needs plays an important role in supporting the necessary "mothering" that is essential during infancy to insure healthy childrearing interactions between mother and child.

Although the newborn does not know or recognize his mother during the first weeks of life, the development of the child begins at this time and the months to follow. This phase in the developmental process is called the "imprinting stage," the time when a mother's smiling face, support, comfort and love and the pleasurable experience of nursing the newborn infant contributes to a secure tension-reducing experience in which there is mutual satisfaction and enjoyment. This type of mother-child relationship produces a consistent, need-satisfying experience for the child that makes it possible for him to similarly respond in adult life.

Scientific appreciation of the neonate's remarkable capacities for social interaction have been documented by the works of Claus and Kennell of Western Reserve University School of Medicine. The authors have emphasized the importance of early parent-infant "bonding" that can prevent both psychological and physical complications after childbirth.

Recent studies validate the importance of unrestricted interaction between parents and newborns during the "sensitive" first few hours after birth. Parents who had extended contact with their newborns immediately postpartum were found to have more extensive verbal interchange with their children two years later. Mothers whose contact with their newborns was increased beyond normal hospital contacts during the first thirty minutes postpartum were found three months later to spend more time fondling and kissing their babies than a control group of mothers who spend more time cleaning their babies. The antiquated hospital policy of separation and minimal contact between mother and infant after birth to prevent infection and manage physical problems may well have interfered with early maternal-infant bonding.

It would appear that dysfunction of the family and the weaknesses of the family bonds may well be related to the old practice of separating mother and baby after birth and the exclusion of the father during the labor and subsequent delivery of the infant. Present-day active participation of both parents during pregnancy, delivery and the early infancy period may well be an important early proper parenting technique to encourage parent-infant bonding. Any definite program aimed at helping to eliminate child abuse must begin with education and training of expectant parents. The parenting programs should not be geared solely to the physical aspects of pregnancy and the birth of the baby, but should contain explanations of the emotional and psychological impact the pregnancy and birth will have for the mother and the father. Future parents should be made aware as to what pregnancy means to them, and how the nurturing of the newborn infant will impact on their own lifestyle. While a doctor or nurse can certainly handle the physical aspects of such an educational program, the discussions around the feelings of the participants should be led by a psychiatrist, a psychologist, or a social worker. Such a team effort can only have positive results if conducted consistently and followed through in the home after the baby's birth.

The hospital setting offers the single best opportunity to teach parents about baby care, give them advice on how to manage life with an infant, and refer them to follow-up community parenting services as needed. New York State instituted a program called the Pre and Postnatal Parent Education Hospital Program, or PPPEHP, which is a statewide effort to reach every family expecting or caring for a newborn baby. PPPEHP is a team approach to parent education and self-help that uses hospital-based health and human services professionals to teach parents about basic baby care, offer instruction on the many adjustments required to manage life as a new parent, and refer families to community-based parenting programs.

For many years it has been the goal of most child advocates to enable *every* young mother in this country to receive not only adequate pre- and postnatal care but a complete program of parenting education and support. If we can reach them at this critical point of their lives, we can do a lot to reduce infant mortality as well as abuse and neglect. The program is designed to promote hospital participation in the delivery of parent education and support services and forge partnerships between hospitals and community-based programs for parents.

In summary: Improvements are necessary to make the delivery of child care services in this country more effective and appropriate, especially in dealing with the prenatal and postnatal care of "high risk" mothers. All urban or poor populations have an increased maternal and infant morbidity and mortality rate which is oftentimes coupled with inadequate medical preventive services and the attitudinal cultural barriers that impede the delivery of these services to the recipients. We must therefore develop child abuse preventive programs for the high-risk population, the underprivileged, the handicapped, the drug addicted, the alcoholics, the woefully immature and the unwed single parents. The encouraged participation of these parents in early preventive programs that offer human support services will ensure that quality of life for child and parents that will not incite parental misbehavior.

Prevention is a community responsibility and one of the most effective means of alleviating child abuse in this country. Education, particularly for parents, will reduce the massive alienation of parents and children which causes family crisis, breakdown, intrafamilialial violence, and subsequent child abuse.

TREATMENT OF CHILD ABUSE

Caring for the maltreating parents was in the past considered a social service responsibility and essentially the burden of the public and private social work agencies. However, traditional social work intervention in caring for these parents has not been totally effective. With the increased awareness and knowledge of why and how child maltreatment occurs, there has been an increased interest and involvement by other professionals and paraprofessionals in public and private social child-caring agencies, child protective societies, and hospitals. A variety of innovative crisis intervention programs staffed by various disciplines with different techniques are providing effective therapeutic models. There is no evidence at present to indicate that any one therapeutic approach to the treatment of abusive parents is more effective than another for a select group of patients.

There are no easy answers to the problems of parenting, especially when dealing with the abusive or neglectful parent. Expertise and time are required to unravel the causative factors. Social and environmental factors may be found which, though objectively undesirable, are not necessarily responsible for the parent's malfunctioning. The adverse social factors may be the result of the parent's psychological state rather than the cause. If the physician lacks training, time, and interest to ascertain which factors are responsible for the child abuse situation, an evaluation by a social worker, psychologist, psychiatric social worker, or psychiatrist is critical. Without this type of data, it is impossible to develop a rational program to prevent further abuse and neglect.

Ideally, each parent should have an intervention plan developed for her based upon an assessment of a number of factors which include:

1. The factors responsible for the parent's dysfunction.
2. The severity of the parent's psychopathology.
3. The overall prognosis for achieving adequate mothering.

4. Time estimated to achieve meaningful change in the mother's ability to mother.
5. Whether the parent's dysfunction is confined to this infant or involves all of her children.
6. The extent to which the mother's malfunctioning extends to her roles, i.e., wife, homemaker, housekeeper.
7. The extent to which the parent's overall malfunctioning, if this is the case, is acute or chronic (reflects a lifelong pattern).
8. The extent to which the mother's malfunctioning is confined to infants as opposed to older children.
9. The parent's willingness to participate in the intervention plan.
10. The availability of personnel and physical resources to implement the various intervention strategies.
11. The risk of the child's sustaining physical abuse by remaining in the home.

All of the above sounds most impersonal, yet it is all aimed at helping the persons involved in child abuse situations. No help can be given to a parent until the situation is recognized for what it is and brought to the attention of those who can help. It all comes down to treating the two victims involved—the abusing parent and the abused child.

Many programs have been developed throughout the country to rehabilitate mother and/or father and protect the child. A temporary shelter program for abusive parents was founded in 1972 at the New York Foundling Hospital Center for Parent and Child Development in New York City.

The program utilizes the best treatment approaches known to date in a residential setting so as not to separate the child from the mother. This model program stresses (1) protection of the child without actual separation from the parents and (2) a rehabilitation or parenting program for the parent.

The advantages of the residential component are the following:

1. It is the only way to observe the interaction between parent and child twenty-four hours a day, seven days a week.
2. It is the best way to diagnose the severity of the problem.
3. It makes possible the formulation of a more realistic treatment plan.
4. It avoids the trauma of separation of child from parent.

5. It enables the parent to establish a meaningful relationship with a caring staff due to the regularity of contacts.

The treatment methods that are utilized in this program are:

1. Paraprofessionals with similar cultural characteristics as the clients who have been found to be effective in communicating and achieving positive results. These paraprofessionals are used in two positions:
    a. Group Mothers who provide the role model in assisting the abusive parent in caring for the child. Group mothers also instruct the mother in preparing meals, handling children's tantrums and ways of responding to a child's physical and emotional needs.
    b. Social Service Assistants. (This idea is modeled after the lay therapist concept.) These paraprofessionals have the major responsibility in "mothering the mother" in an attempt to fulfill her unmet dependency needs and provide a "lifeline" which the parent can utilize in times of stress. When the mothers are ready to leave the shelter, the social service assistants help them in securing better apartments, help them find jobs or job training, and teach them how to use community resources. The social service assistants make periodic visits to the homes and are available to the mothers in an emergency crisis situation.
2. Educational activities in the program are aimed toward teaching mothers responsibilities in terms of their roles in meeting the physical and emotional needs of the child. Activities include courses on human sexuality, child growth and development, and the child's medical needs. Consumer education sessions, given by a member of the Home Economics Department of Hunter College, are aimed at giving the mother some experience in family budgeting and intelligent shopping.
3. A Therapeutic Nursery for infants: Parents learn how to provide for the needs of the child in play sessions under the supervision of an Early Childhood Development expert. A videotape feedback confrontation technique is used to affect the behavior of the children by enlisting the mother's help as therapist. With the use of video feedback, the opportunity to record a segment of typical interaction during a play and feeding session between parent and

child can immediately be used to confront the mother with her own pattern of reacting. With such highly relevant and appropriate data available immediately after the occurrence, the learning impact is enhanced. This has proven to be an important modality in effecting behavior modification.

4. After Care. This is a very important aspect of the program. The mother with her child remains in the shelter residential program for six to ten months. If it is determined that she has made progress and benefited from the program, she is discharged to community living with her child. The mother and child attend the after care program for one year or more. She is visited in her home at least twice a week by her social service assistant who is continuously on call for an emergency. She returns to the center for individual and group therapy, and is visited once a week at home by a visiting nurse.

In summary: This model program is an innovative approach to the problem of child maltreatment combining psychiatric, medical, and social services in the treatment of the parents and the child.

OBJECTIVES OF CHILD ABUSE PREVENTIVE AND TREATMENT PROGRAMS

1. To prevent separation of parents and child whenever possible.
2. To prevent the placement of children in institutions.
3. To encourage the attainment of self-care status on the part of parents.
4. To stimulate the attainment of self-sufficiency for the family unit.
5. To prevent further abuse or neglect by removing children from families who show an unwillingness or inability to profit from the treatment program.

There are seven components to the Model Program at the Foundling Hospital in New York City:

1. Multidisciplinary team approach—professionals and paraprofessionals.
2. Engagement of the surrogate mothers as "lay therapists."
3. 24 hour, 7 days a week "hot line" or "lifeline" service for crisis situations.

4. In-resident facility for mother and child.
5. "Half-way House"—Agency Operated Boarding Home for mothers and children.
6. Outpatient "I Care" program providing family supportive services.
7. Nursery providing play therapy, crisis intervention, and pediatric services.

It has been conclusively proven that parent rehabilitation is possible in the majority of cases. Effective therapeutic approaches assure both child and parent of a positive and satisfying relationship. The work done to rehabilitate abusive parents may be slow and tedious, but it is certainly effective and worthwhile.

LEGAL RESPONSIBILITIES

Constructive use of the laws governing society should safeguard the rights of the abused child, parent, and physician. Immediate assistance must be made available to the abused child by the appropriate community and child welfare services. The utilization of law enforcement agents and the criminal court are to be considered if the child is a victim of "battering" by a parent leading to hospitalization or to death. Law enforcement agents should also be informed if appropriate child protective agencies are not available in the community. The results of severe abusive parental injury on a child often require the prompt removal of the victim from the life-threatening and hazardous home environment. In certain states, children's aid societies and The Society for the Prevention of Cruelty to Children have taken on the responsibilities of providing maximum immediate protection for any maltreated child.

The family and criminal courts are available to review petitions for child placement or parental prosecutions. The courts also protect the parents through the acceptance of evidence against the parents that is only beyond any reasonable doubt.

The physicians are the first line of defense in the fight to decrease the incidence of the maltreatment syndrome in children. In order that this can be fully accomplished, they must be legally free to report and take positive responsible action to protect the abused child with no fear of possible personal or professional reprisal.

The Advisory Committee to the Children's Division of The American Humane Association strongly urged that state legislation be proposed making it mandatory to report cases of suspected inflicted injuries on children. The passage of such a law in all states has aided in case findings and has assured safety to the victims of childhood neglect and abuse. The Committee recommended:

1. That such legislation be directed to medical practitioners and hospital personnel coming in contact with children for the purpose of examination and treatment of injuries sustained allegedly from accidental or other causes.

2. That doctors and hospital personnel have mandatory responsibility for reporting all cases of child injury where medical diagnosis and findings are incompatible with alleged history of how injuries were sustained and the syndrome leads to the inference of "inflicted injuries."

3. That doctors and hospital staff members reporting cases of suspected inflicted injuries be made immune to possible civil or criminal action for the disclosure of matters which might be considered confidential because of the doctor-patient relationship.

4. That all reports of cases of suspected inflicted injuries be made to the public or voluntary child welfare service which carries the child protective function in the community.

Protective agencies must relate to the judicial authority in the community, and is through these courts that plans are made to adequately care for the neglected or abused child.

Many authorities in the field of child protection feel that a law making it mandatory to report child neglect and abuse is not an absolute necessity in the prevention of the problem. They feel that the moral obligation of all those responsible for the care of children, including physicians, hospital administrators, nurses, social service workers, and child care professionals, should dictate the necessity of bringing these children to the attention of the child protective agencies. The law, however, serves the purpose of lessening the fears of those mandated to report suspected brutality to children.

Those interested in the legal aspects of the problem of maltreatment of children have questioned the type of legal authority granted by the law in the protection of the child. It is stressed by many that punitive aspects of such a law should be minimized, and they advocate the exclusion of the law as part of a criminal act. Treatment and prevention programs have documented that with the provision of needed human support services parents can be motivated and helped in keeping their families intact. Retributive or punitive action toward the parents, without thought of rehabilitation, yields little benefit for the children involved.

The selection of a community child protective agency to which a physician should report his or her case of child abuse or neglect should offer statewide coverage and have authority to investigate and to initiate appropriate legal action. It should have staff sufficient in number and training to conduct an effective investigation twenty-four-hour-a-day, seven-day-a-week service on an emergency basis as the need arises. Time is of the essence and every hour may mean the possible loss of life. For this reason, the agency to which the cases of child maltreatment are to be reported according to law must be provided with the necessary facilities, tools, and personnel to fulfill their function. These facilities and services must be available immediately and must be ready to meet the wide range of problems involved in the maltreatment syndrome of children.

All steps must first be taken to protect the child by whatever means possible but, at the same time, steps must also be taken to protect parents from facing unfair punishment and criminal prosecution. This punitive action does not correct the underlying cause of the abuse. The psychodynamics involved in their abusive actions should be studied and evaluated before any prosecution and punishment is undertaken.

If criminal prosecution of parents is prematurely used, it may prevent parents from seeking medical attention soon enough, or perhaps not at all, for fear of legal entanglement and possible criminal prosecution. In other words, it may motivate failure to get medical help until the situation becomes critical and a child's welfare may be jeopardized. There have been documented cases where parents explain that their failure to give prompt medical attention was due to fear of prosecution. These cases have apparently occurred in communities where child protective services were not available and reporting to the police was the customary procedure.

If a community agency or a child protective group cannot make the environmental changes necessary for the security of the neglected and abused child, then these agencies must appeal to the courts for their cooperative assistance. The social service workers and/or the child protective agencies, after investigations, may petition the courts for assistance in removing the child from the parents. Such a court may be a special family court created to handle only matters relating to children, or it may be a special part of a county, district, or probate court. In some jurisdictions, it is a specialized court with broad jurisdiction covering marital or family problems as a domestic relations court, a juvenile court, or a family court. Most of the juvenile courts have exclusive jurisdiction over neglected or delinquent children within age limits prescribed by law in each state.

A successful criminal prosecution of the guilty parent is often difficult even in those cases where it has led to death of the child. Practically all of these crimes are committed behind closed doors and "shuttered" windows making it almost impossible to prove beyond a reasonable doubt that the crime was committed by the parent. Only in cases of manslaughter when a parent confesses to the crime of child beating and death is the perpetrator of the action punished. For this reason, civil proceedings are encouraged wherein the preponderance of evidence and the concept of *res ipsa loquitur* may be applied as an effective means of protecting the abused child by removal from the parents. In civil justice, the medical evidences of child abuse (photographs of injuries, x-rays, and other objective evidence) are accepted by the courts as strong testimony that the injuries sustained by the child "speak for themselves." Judge Harold A. Felix of the Family Court of the State of New York established a precedent when he rendered his opinion in a case of child abuse by stating:

> Therefore, in this type of proceeding affecting a battered child syndrome, I am borrowing from the evidentiary law of negligence the principle of *res ipsa loquitur* and accepting the proposition that the condition of the child speaks for itself, thus permitting an inference of neglect to be drawn from proof of the child's age and condition and that the latter is such as in the ordinary course of things does not happen if the parent who has the responsibility and control of an infant is protective and nonabusive.

It is the basic philosophy in all these courts that justice for children is given first consideration, followed by parental therapy as a substitution for legal punishment. The family court's attitude at present considers what is "in the best interests of the child."

The medical and social problems involved have become more fully understood in recent years, but unfortunately, there has been a lack of keeping pace with this problem by the courts. In the past, cases of gross neglect and abuse have been referred to the courts and, in view of insufficient evidence, the child has been returned to the parents. It is certainly most difficult to prove inflicted injury by the parents, since this malicious abuse is usually done without any witnesses. The court is naturally guided by the dictum "the child belongs to the mother, and the mother belongs to the child." In a great many of these cases where the courts have decided to return the child to an offending parent, these children have again been brought to hospitals with inflicted trauma— many of them close to death.

Paulsen has emphasized that leaving a child in his home, when he bears the marks of unusual injuries which seem to have been intentionally inflicted, is taking a chance with the child's life. He further states: "Not all doubts should be resolved in favor of parents. Those who seek a court order to remove a child from a dangerous situation should not have to disprove every plausible explanation of the child's wounds. Parents have a right to their children, but their children have a right to live."

In view of our recent experiences with child abuse cases and the courts, it should be the responsibility of the courts to evaluate more closely the reports of the social service workers and the objective medical evidence presented by the physician before making a decision on the advisability of returning the child to an environment which may prove hazardous. The courts should also recognize the needs of the parents involved in this type of problem and be aware of the community services that are available to them for therapeutic guidance and counseling.

If removal is considered by the courts, with social planning to be in the best interest of the child, then definitive steps are taken to have the child placed in a foster home or other child-caring institutions with available trained child care and social service personnel. It cannot be too strongly stressed that removal of the child at this time by the court should serve two purposes: first, rehabilitation of the parents in order to properly receive the child once again; second, removal of the child until the home is made a better and more secure place in which to live.

This entire problem of treating and preventing neglect and abuse of children depends on the cooperative efforts of all disciplines, the social, medical, and legal agencies and personnel who are responsible for the health and welfare of children. Integrated multidisciplinary coordinated treatment modalities should be available in every community. The court's recommendations cannot be carried out in areas where facilities and services for children simply do not exist. Voluntary and public agencies must be made available to provide shelter care, detention care, institutional or foster care and homemakers for these families when so ordered by the court. Only in this way can these children be adequately protected from future neglect and abuse, and the parents given the assistance and therapeutic help that can lead to better parental care.

In the process of protecting children, the court must maintain objectivity on the basis of evidence produced and judged without assuming the role of a social worker, psychiatrist, or family counselor. All information from the children's social service agencies and the child protective agency in the community, in conjunction with the physician's diagnostic medical evidence, should be made available to serve the courts with the facts necessary for rendering a decision without any unnecessary time-consuming prolongation of neglect cases.

In summary: Protection and prevention of the neglect and abuse of children rests upon the concise and complete casework services by the child protective agencies exploring the complaints of abuse or neglect. Medical diagnosis is added to the evaluation of the abuse and/or neglect findings which are then presented for the action of the courts to evaluate the standards of child care in the particular family. If the child's needs are best served by the immediate removal from the family, a neglect petition is filed. Acceptance of the petition by the court begins the judicial process which leads to curtailment or nullification of parental rights in the best interests of the children.

It has been stated that no law can be better than its implementation, and its implementation can be no better than the resources permit. Preventive and therapeutic mental health community services for the parents must be made available. Child-caring institutions, trained social workers, foster homes, homemakers, and day care centers are necessary if the plight of the maltreated child is to be improved.

Chapter 7

THE LEGAL FRAMEWORK
FOR CHILD PROTECTION

For too long, child maltreatment was a hidden problem, relegated to understaffed and overwhelmed protective agencies far from public view. Only in recent years has the true seriousness of child abuse and child neglect been widely recognized.

In the 1960s, the plight of the "battered child" was brought to public attention, largely through the efforts of leaders in the medical profession. Legislative action quickly followed. In 1963, the United States Children's Bureau published a guide for child abuse legislation, based on the new concept of reporting child abuse to a state central register of records. In the context of the times, the 1963 Model Child Protection Act was an innovative document. Within three years, every state enacted a reporting law, many patterned after the Children's Bureau model.

By the 1970s, widespread concern over endangered children had broadened to include all elements of the "Maltreatment Syndrome" so that over forty states had amended their laws to require the reporting of suspected child neglect as well as child abuse. Reporting laws were also expanded to include important ancillary provisions for immunity for good faith reporting, penalities for failure to report, protective custody and the abrogation of certain privileged communications. Over thirty states have laws which establish a central register of reports, and an increasing number of states are legislatively prescribing procedures for case handling and case management.

The Federal Child Abuse Prevention and Treatment Act of 1974 reflected this evolution toward improved and expanded child protective laws. Its original eligibility criteria for state grants described the essential fundamentals of an effective statewide child protection system. Section 4 (b) (2) of the Act provided:

> (2) In order for a State to qualify for assistance under this subsection, such State shall:
>
> (A) have in effect a State child abuse and neglect law which shall include

provisions for immunity for persons reporting instances of child abuse and neglect from prosecution, under any State or local law, arising out of such reporting;

(B) provide for the reporting of known and suspected instances of child abuse and neglect;

(C) provide that upon receipt of a report of known or suspected instances of child abuse or neglect an investigation shall be initiated promptly to substantiate the accuracy of the report, and, upon a finding of abuse or neglect, immediate steps shall be taken to protect the health and welfare of the abused or neglected child, as well as that of any other child under the same care who may be in danger of abuse or neglect;

(D) demonstrate that there are in effect throughout the State, in connection with the enforcement of child abuse and neglect laws and with the reporting of suspected instances of child abuse and neglect, such administrative procedures, such personnel trained in child abuse and neglect prevention and treatment, such training procedures, such institutional and other facilities (public and private), and such related multidisciplinary programs and services as may be necessary or appropriate to assure that the State will deal effectively with child abuse and neglect cases in the State;

(E) provide for methods to preserve the confidentiality of all records in order to protect the rights of the child, his parents or guardians;

(F) provide for the cooperation of law enforcement officials, courts of competent jurisdiction, and appropriate State agencies providing human services;

(G) provide that in every case involving an abused or neglected child which results in a judicial proceeding a guardian *ad litem* shall be appointed to represent the child in such proceeding;

(H) provide that the aggregate of support for programs or projects related to child abuse and neglect assisted by State funds shall not be reduced below the level provided during fiscal year 1973, and set forth policies and procedures designed to assure that Federal funds made available under this Act for any fiscal year will be so used as to supplement and, to the extent practicable, increase the level of State funds which would, in the absence of Federal funds, be available for such programs and projects;

(I) provide for dissemination of information to the general public with respect to the problem of child abuse and neglect and the facilities and prevention and treatment methods available to combat instances of child abuse and neglect; and

(J) to the extent feasible, insure that parental organizations combating child abuse and neglect receive preferential treatment.

Although these requirements merely stated the indispensable fundamentals of an effective child protective system, a number of states had difficulty implementing them because they often required substantial legislative and programmatic upgrading. The provisions of the Model Child Protection Act reflect and conform to the requirements for state eligibility originally specified in the Federal Child Abuse Prevention and Treatment Act. Although a state may be deemed eligible for a state grant without enacting the provisions of the Model Act, the Model Act was designed so that any state adopting it would automatically satisfy the state law requirements of the federal law. (However, the Model Act cannot deal with those issues of eligibility involving programmatic and procedural requirements.)

Although the Model Act was initially intended to assist states seeking to meet federal eligibility requirements, its provisions go beyond the minimum requirements in the federal law. The Model Act is being offered as a living instrument to assist *all* states seeking to improve the necessary legal framework for an effective and fair child protection system.

PHILOSOPHY OF THE MODEL ACT

Abused and neglected children are in urgent need of protection. But there are no provisions in the Model Act for punishment, because in most situations criminal intent is not present. The purposes of the Act are curative and remedial.

Child maltreatment is primarily caused by social and psychological ills. The best way to protect a child is to deal with these underlying ills. Often, a family's ability to care for and protect its children can be strengthened by appropriate treatment and ameliorative services.

Unfortunately, however, families frequently do not seek help on their own. Hence, the Model Act attempts to assist and encourage parents to seek help in meeting their child care responsibilities. But if parents do not act on their own, some third person must take protective action. In the past, though, many private citizens and professionals failed to report substantial numbers of children whose condition indicated that they were abused or neglected. Therefore, the Model Act seeks to encourage fuller reporting by establishing simplified reporting procedures and by establishing a fair and effective state and local child protection system that can handle the increased reports that will result. In each county a child protective service is established to swiftly and competently investigate reports of known or suspected child abuse and neglect, while maintaining due process and fundamental fairness to parents.

The most important aspect of the Model Act is its emphasis on the development of services to go along with increased reporting. It would have been far easier—there would have been less work and less controversy

—if only a reporting law were proposed. But to do so would be to ignore the increased reports that inevitably flow from an improved reporting law. Unless a system for handling these increased reports is established, strengthening reporting requirements and improving reporting techniques can work to the detriment of agency and family welfare.

Whenever a family needs services, the Model Act requires that such services be offered first on a voluntary basis. The protective agency is to resort to court only if necessary. [See sections 16(g), (h), (j), and (k).] When the powers of a court must be invoked to protect a child, the Model Act favors resort to a civil proceeding in a family or juvenile court. Though referral to a criminal court may be appropriate in certain situations, the criminal court can protect a child only by jailing an offending parent. The juvenile court, on the other hand, can help provide social and psychological services necessary to deal with some of the fundamental problems which lead to abuse and neglect.

Ultimately, however, efforts to preserve and improve family stability are, and must remain, the province of community resources and agencies with a broader and more long-range responsibility towards children and families than that of a public, child protective service agency. The Model Act does not seek to shift this fundamental social welfare responsibility away from community resources and agencies already involved successfully in helping children and families nor does it seek to discourage the development of additional community-based treatment and prevention programs. Indeed, through its provisions for a community child protection advisory board, interdisciplinary teams, a local plan for child protective services, and the authorization for the child protective service to purchase the services of other agencies, the Model Act seeks to encourage existing agencies to assume greater treatment responsibility and to expand their treatment capacity.

Finally, the Model Act recognizes that institutional child abuse and neglect is more widespread than we would like to believe. Therefore, the Act makes provision for the appropriate handling of reports of the abuse and neglect of children who live in public and private *residential* facilities.

Emphasis on Self-Help and Voluntarily Sought Services

In the United States, there has been a traditional and fundamental reliance on self-help for personal problems and on voluntarily sought social and child welfare services. Key to the effectiveness of any child protection system is its ability to offer services on a voluntary basis. From practical and humanitarian points of view, it is preferable that families needing help seek it on their own. Experience has shown that services are more effective when sought or accepted voluntarily—many parents will seek out help, or will accept it when it is offered, if they understand their need for it. Parents must be assisted and encouraged to find the help they need.

The Model Act reaffirms this traditional and fundamental reliance on voluntarily sought social and child welfare services by encouraging parents to seek help through the procedures and agencies established by the Act and through other means as well. Examples of such assistance include traditional family counseling and mental health services, and such newer, specialized resources for families in trouble as: Parents Anonymous; hotlines, helplines, and other telephone counseling services; child development, parent effectiveness, and infant stimulation centers; and crisis nurseries and drop-in services. Thus, for example, Section 3 is careful to ensure that parents calling on the statewide hotline who need assistance will be directed to those services that seem most appropriate for them.

Unified Definition of "Child Abuse and Neglect"

The increased formality and legal strictures surrounding contemporary child protection work require that the terms "child abuse" and "child neglect" be clearly and carefully defined to meet the objectives they are meant to serve. The definitions of "child abuse" and "child neglect" used in the Model Act unify all forms of child maltreatment (including child battering, physical attack, dependency, abandonment, and failure to provide food, clothing, shelter, and other necessities) in one conceptual framework—the "abused or neglected child."

Artificially created distinctions between "child abuse" and "child neglect" can cause harmful differences in the handling of cases. But, as made clear by the concept of the "maltreatment syndrome," the harm done to a child because of inadequate parental care can be just as severe and long lasting as the harm caused by physical battering. Indeed, child abuse and child neglect often occur together and are interrelated problems falling, in large part, within the concept of the "maltreated child." (See section 4.)

Even before passage of the Federal Child Abuse Prevention and

Treatment Act of 1974, which required states to provide for the reporting of child neglect as well as abuse in order to receive special grants, all states were broadening the circumstances requiring a report. Most states had concluded that physical abuse, child battering, sexual abuse, child neglect, abandonment, emotional abuse and emotional neglect are all aspects of the same problem—the inadequate parental care of children. They had realized that to single out one form of maltreatment for special attention would be to establish false and dangerously misleading distinctions. Child neglect can be as damaging and just as deadly as child abuse.

As a result of these and other changes, most states have experienced phenomenal increases in the number of reports of known and suspected child abuse and child neglect. But it is important to note that broadening the circumstances that must be reported does not necessarily increase the actual number of cases brought to the attention of the authorities. It may mean only that cases which were once handled outside the mandated reporting process—by police, welfare agencies, child protective agencies, and courts—are now handled within it.

Reporting of Known and Suspected Child Abuse and Neglect

When parents faced with child abuse and child neglect problems do not seek help on their own, the responsibility to take protective action rests with others. But before social service and other helping agencies can assist children and parents, they must learn of the child's predicament. Someone—a friend, a neighbor, a relative, or a concerned professional—must recognize the child's danger and report it. If a case of suspected child abuse or child neglect is not reported, a protective agency cannot become involved, emergency protective measures cannot be taken, and a treatment plan cannot be developed.

Although the early recognition and reporting of suspected child abuse and neglect are the first essential steps in preventing further maltreatment, many physicians, nurses, social workers, teachers and others do not report the abuse or neglect that they see. Because of the reluctance of many professionals to take action to protect children, all states have passed laws that require, under penalty, certain professionals to report known and suspected child abuse and neglect.

The medical professional was the first, and remains the foremost, target of these reporting statutes. But the early focus on physicians (who were considered the professionals most likely to see injured children) quickly expanded to include all professionals in the healing arts, and has since broadened to include teachers, social workers, police, clergymen and coroners, among others. In addition, an increasing number of states (over twenty at this writing) require "any person" to report known and suspected child abuse and neglect.

The Model Act continues this approach by requiring certain professionals to report, because of their frequent contact with children and because their training and experience should make them sensitive to possible abuse and neglect in the children they see. [See section 5.] In addition, all persons are permitted to report when they have reasonable cause to suspect that a child is abused or neglected. [See section 6.]

State reporting laws are most notable for what they do *not* require. They do not require that the individual making the report be certain a child is abused or neglected. They require only that the individual "suspect," "reasonably suspect," "have reason to believe," or "have cause to believe" that a child is abused or neglected. Under the Model Act, specified professionals must report if they have *"reasonable cause to suspect"* that a child is abused or neglected. This statutory language is intended to ensure the fullest possible reporting of appropriate situations.

"Reasonable cause to suspect" can include the nature of the child's injuries, the history of prior injuries to a child, the condition of a child, his personal hygiene and his clothing, the statements and demeanor of a child or parent (especially if the injuries to the child are at variance to the parental explanation of them), the condition of the home, and the statements of others.

Because in the past cumbersome and confusing reporting procedures have discouraged more complete reporting, the Model Act is careful to establish simple and easy to use reporting procedures. [See section 13.]

After a report is made, the child protective agency is responsible for determining the child's true condition and for beginning the process of diagnosis, protection, and treatment.

Protective Custody

In most child abuse and neglect situations, the child does not have to be removed from his parents' custody in order to protect his well-being and future development. Indeed, in many situations, removal may be harmful to the child. The child may see separation from his parents as a deprivation or as a punishment for the child's inadequacy. Removal may be counterproductive to any treatment effort; it may destroy the fragile family fabric and make it more difficult for the parents to cope with the child when he is returned to their care. Moreover, the conditions of substitute care are also often unsuitable for the child's optimum care and development.

However, sometimes a child has to be removed from his home against parental wishes for his own safety. Often such removal must occur before court action is possible, because the child may be further harmed during the time necessary to obtain a court order. In most states, the police are already authorized to take children into protective custody, either through specific child protective legislation or their general law enforcement powers. Over the years the right of physicians and social workers to place children in protective custody has gained wide acceptance. The Model Act continues such procedures. [See section 9.]

Nevertheless, there is always the danger of careless or automatic— though well-meaning—exercise of the power to place a child in protective custody. In too many situations, past practice has been to remove a child from his home first—and to ask questions later. The Model Act seeks to prevent the indiscriminate use of protective custody by imposing two conditions for such emergency protective custody: (1) The child must be in imminent danger, and (2) there must be no time to apply for a court order. Only in such grave and urgent situations may a child be removed without prior court approval. Examples of such situations include the following: when children are being attacked or are in imminent danger of being attacked by their parents; when children need immediate food, clothing, shelter, or medical care; when young children are left alone unattended; or when it appears that the entire family may disappear before the facts can be sorted out. [See section 9(a).]

Because the correctness of the protective custody decision should be reviewed by a court as soon as possible, the Model Act establishes a twenty-four-hour time limit for holding a child without a court order. By that time, there is no reason why a judge cannot be reached. The possibility of disturbing a judge on a weekend is a small price to pay for ensuring that the initial decision is reviewed promptly. [See sections 9(d) and (e).]

Immunity from Liability

Immunity from liability for reporting in good faith is essential to any child protective system which must rely on third party reporting. Otherwise, fears of unjust lawsuits for libel, slander, defamation, invasion of privacy, or breach of confidentiality may discourage reporting. Even though good faith on the part of the reporter would probably be a defense against such lawsuits, all states specifically grant mandated reporters immunity from civil liability for good faith reports in order to eradicate all vestiges of uncertainty; all but one also grant immunity from criminal liability. Like a growing number of states, and in accordance with the Federal Child Abuse Prevention and Treatment Act, [Section 4(b) (2) (A)], the Model Act extends this specific grant of immunity to *any person* acting in good faith, whether or not mandated by law to report. Immunity exists only when someone is acting in "good faith." Someone who makes a malicious report would lose this grant of immunity. [See section 10.]

Because fear of lawsuits is frequently cited as a deterrent to more complete reporting, this immunity provision should be clearly explained in any public and professional education campaign about the law. [See section 26.]

Abrogation of Privileged Communications

Child abuse and child neglect usually occur behind closed doors without witnesses. In establishing that a child has been abused and neglected, great reliance is necessarily placed on medical evidence and on the statements of the child and parents. Conversations between parents and many of the professionals most likely to learn about child abuse, such as those between doctor and patient or social worker and client, are statutorily made "privileged communications." Ordinarily, anyone subject to such a privilege is prohibited by law from divulging anything told to them by the protected person, unless permission is given. While a legal mandate to report known and suspected child abuse and neglect automatically overrides any other law about privileged communication, there are many situations where concern over the privileged nature of a communication could become an obstacle to reporting. For example, physicians might think that they could not make a report about suspicious injuries without first securing the permission of the parents.

Therefore, for purposes of reporting, cooperating with the child protective services, and testifying in court about known or suspected child abuse or neglect, the Model Act abrogates the husband-wife privilege and all professional privileges except the attorney-client privilege. Although this abrogation is absolute, protective workers, judges, and prosecutors should use it with discretion, especially in situations involving spouses and treatment professionals who may have a trustful relationship with the parents. [See section 11.]

Penalties for Failure to Report

Although the ultimate success of a child protective reporting system must depend upon the willing cooperation of professionals and private citizens, reporting requirements need enforceable provisions for the few who refuse to accept their legal and moral obligations to protect endangered children. Thus, the reporting laws of over half the states contain specific criminal and civil penalty clauses for failure to report. The Model Act also has one, although it limits penalties to situations in which there has been a "knowing and willful failure" to fulfill the legal obligation to report. This is meant to protect those professionals who make a careful and reasoned decision against reporting a particular situation. Only professionals mandated to make reports are subject to this penalty for failure to report. [See section 12.]

Besides acting to encourage fuller reporting, penalty clauses assist mandated reporters in working with parents. They make it easier for doctors, teachers, social workers, day care workers, and others to explain to parents why they are making a report. In addition, experience shows that a penalty clause is invaluable to staff members of agencies and institutions who must often persuade their superiors of the necessity of making a report. (For example, nurses frequently complain that only mention of the penalty clause convinces hospital administrators to commence protective action.)

Although penalty provisions are a valuable and necessary component of an effective reporting law, it must be emphasized that the main reason for underreporting remains ignorance and misunderstanding of the reporting law and of child protective procedures. The most effective way to encourage full and accurate reporting is through professional and public education about the nature of child abuse and neglect. Citizens, but especially professionals, including child care professionals, physicians, nurses, social workers, and teachers must be made sensitive to the occurrence of child abuse and neglect, must be able to identify it, and must know how to report it. [See section 26.]

Photographs and X-rays

X-rays can be crucial to early and accurate diagnosis of child abuse and neglect. They can also play a crucial role in preserving evidence. Long after memories have faded, photographs and X-rays can provide extra assurance that subsequent child protective decision-making, and possible court action, reflect the severity of the child's initial condition, particularly when case records lack sufficient detail. A photograph or an X-ray can be worth, as the cliché goes, a thousand words. Therefore, the Model Act authorizes persons and officials required to report to take, or arrange to have taken, photographs and X-rays without parental permission, which would otherwise be required in many circumstances. [See section 8.]

Statewide Twenty-four-hour-a-day Reporting Hot Line

In the past, the difficulty of making reports was one of the major stumbling blocks to more complete reporting. To facilitate the reporting process, the Model Act creates a twenty-four-hour-a-day, seven-day-a-week, toll-free telephone number to accept reports of known and suspected child abuse and neglect. The single statewide number is meant to encourage reporting by simplifying the reporting process and by making it widely accessible. It creates one easily publicized phone number for an entire state. Since the number is statewide, some people using it would have to pay for a long distance call; having a toll-free number avoids this obstacle to reporting. The number should be available twenty-four-hours-a-day because emergencies arise at all hours. States that already have such a system report there is sufficient use of the telephone number throughout the day and night to justify this procedure. [See section 13.]

Specialized Local Child Protective Agency

Strengthening reporting requirements can be detrimental to the functioning of agencies and the welfare of families unless a system is established to respond to the reports. The Model Act creates a child protective system capable of investigating reports swiftly and competently while maintaining due process and fundamental fairness to parents. [See sections 14, 15 and 16.]

Until the late 1970s, insufficient attention was paid to establishing strong, viable local child protective agencies. Responsibility for the prompt and effective handling of reports dispersed among a number of public agencies which had many other, often conflicting, duties which competed for scarce resources and attention.

Because most acts of abuse or neglect happen in the privacy of the home without any witnesses, gathering information on what happened can be exceedingly difficult. If the parents are looking for help, they may tell the worker what happened, but often they deny everything the worker has learned from others. Protective caseworkers have great difficulty in getting genuine information about families, and often they are unsure of their role and responsibilities in protecting children. Many agencies are plagued with staff turnovers as high as 100 percent every year or so. The staggering responsibilities placed on protective caseworkers, and the unique skills demanded by protective work, require that protective agencies be specialized and have a highly qualified staff.

The Model Act establishes a child protective service agency in each county or comparable political subdivision of a state. The local child protective agency is the heart of the child protective system established by the Model Act. Through the local agency, the Act seeks to focus and strengthen local efforts to improve the prevention and treatment of child abuse and neglect. The existence of a single agency to receive and investigate *all* reports in each community is expected to eliminate the confusion and lack of accountability that can occur when reports are handled by a number of different agencies. In addition, the Model Act looks to the local agency, with the assistance of the Community Child Abuse and Neglect Advisory Board, described in Section 17, to identify gaps in service and to move to fill them. [See section 15.]

It is important to emphasize that no new agency need be established if an existing agency, or part of one, can provide the child protective services required by the Model Act. In states with cither state administered or supervised social service departments, for example, the state department could establish or designate specialized staff units at the county or regional level; or it could choose to designate and purchase the services of another public or private agency, perhaps even sponsoring the creation of an entirely new agency. (The Model Act discourages the designation of police or law enforcement agencies because criminal intent is largely absent in abuse and neglect cases. If a community decides to empower a law enforcement agency to perform the child protective investigation, this agency should establish a specialized unit staffed by nonuniformed officers qualified to deal with the social and family problems which lie at the root of child abuse and neglect, and it should be able to make the type of referrals crucial for the successful handling of cases. Ordinarily, this would be the police youth bureau or sex crimes bureau.) [See section 14.]

The local child protective service is required to receive reports at all hours of the day or night. Investigations must commence within twenty-four hours. Thus, for example, the investigation of a report received on a Friday night must begin no later than Saturday night at the same hour. The child protective service must be able to receive and evaluate reports at all times, and it must be able to provide emergency services immediately when needed. Hence, the person in the agency who receives the report must be able to assess the need for immediate action. An answering service cannot provide this kind of assessment. [See section 16.]

The purpose of the child protective investigation is to protect and enhance the health and welfare of the children and families involved by beginning the process of helping the parents to meet their child care responsibilities. Specifically, the child protective service agency is assigned the crucial first steps of:

(1) providing immediate protection to children, through temporary stabilization of the home environment as well as protective custody;
(2) assessing the needs of children and families;
(3) providing or arranging for protection, treatment, and ameliorative services; and,
(4) when necessary, instituting civil court action (ordinarily juvenile court action) to remove a child from a dangerous environment or to impose treatment on his family.

Even though persons not legally required to report (including friends, neighbors and relatives) make the largest proportion of child protective reports, their reports are sometimes given second class status. Automatic distinctions based on who made a report have no place in child protective efforts; merely because a report is made by a private citizen or nonmandated professional does not make it any less serious than one made by a legally mandated reporter. Reports from every source must be handled with the same care. Of course, the child protective service should establish necessary investigative priorities based upon the actual urgency of the case—but not on the basis of who made the report. [See section 6 and 16(a).]

After receiving a report of suspected child abuse or neglect, the protective agency investigates to determine whether the child is in danger and what services should be offered the family. Protective caseworkers may contact schools, neighbors, relatives, and the source of the report to obtain as complete a picture of the situation as possible. On the basis of these findings as well as interviews with the family, caseworkers evaluate the family and decide what, if anything, must be done to protect the child.

Interdisciplinary Team

Although the Model Act recommends that the child protective agency be a social service agency, no single agency can successfully perform all the important functions assigned to the child protective agency. Optimal diagnostic and treatment efforts require the contributions of a wide range of professionals and community agencies. In many parts of the country, the creation of interdisciplinary teams has succeeded in bringing the collective expertise of relevant professionals to bear in identification and treatment. Thus the Model Act requires the child protective agency to convene "one or more interdisciplinary 'Child Protective Teams' to assist it in its diagnostic, assessment, service, and coordination responsibilities." [See section 16(e).]

Community Child Protection Advisory Board

Decisive to the success of any child protective agency is its ability to engage existing community services in its efforts to create indigenous, responsive prevention and treatment programs. Ultimately, efforts to preserve and improve family stability are, and must remain, the province of community resources and agencies with a broader and more long-range responsibility toward children and families than the child protective service agency. Thus the Model Act creates the Community Child Protection Advisory Board to ensure cooperative planning and evaluation of services for endangered children and their families. [See section 17.]

The Advisory Board has major responsibilities in the formulation of the local plan for child protective services. The plan is expected to be the blueprint to establish a framework of cooperative community structures for services to prevent and treat child abuse and neglect. A key aspect of the plan is the requirement for the broadest possible public and professional consultation *during* its preparation. Part of this consultation is achieved through a public hearing held by the Advisory Board. The local plan should cover all local activities undertaken to fulfill each provision of the state's child abuse and neglect laws. [See section 18.] It is expected that the local plan will include provisions on: the receipt, investigation, and verification of reports; the determination of protection, treatment, and ameliorative service needs; the provision of such services; when necessary, resort to criminal or juvenile court; and monitoring, evaluation, and planning. The local plan should also include full descriptions of staff qualifications, training procedures, institutional or other facilities (public and private), related multidisciplinary programs and services as may be necessary, purchase of service procedures, public and professional education and training programs, cooperative interagency activities, as well as any other relevant efforts.

The provision authorizing the purchase and use of the services of other public or private agencies, it is hoped, will provide the financial backbone of the plan.

State Responsibilities

Sustained efforts at the state level to improve child abuse and neglect services are often all but impossible. Sometimes, only one professional, sometimes titled the "child protection consultant," is assigned to child protective concerns at the state level. Long-range, rational planning cannot be performed in such situations; even responding to day-to-day operational concerns becomes an unmanageable burden. Furthermore, local agencies are forced to fend for themselves, learning from trial and error, instead of benefiting from the informed guidance of state officials. Therefore, the Model Act assigns the state department with social service capabilities a broad mandate to strengthen and improve child abuse and neglect prevention and treatment efforts.

To give the state department real ability to shape the activities of local child protective agencies, the Model Act authorizes the state department to withhold state reimbursement for all or part of the local agency's activities if its annual plan for services is ultimately disapproved.* Of course, this power cannot be exercised lightly. Nor is it an absolute power; the state department's decisions under this section are made reviewable through the state's Civil Procedure Law. [See section 18(f).]

State Child Abuse and Neglect Coordinating Committee

The Model Act also establishes a "State Child Abuse and Neglect Coordinating Committee" to enhance the state department's efforts, while at the same time ensuring consultation, coordination, and cooperation between the state department and other relevant state agencies. [See section 20.]

State Citizens' Committee

The Model Act establishes a "statewide Citizen's Committee on Child Abuse and Neglect" to advise the governor, the state department, and the State Child Abuse and Neglect Coordinating Committee. The Citizen's Committee, made up of persons of distinction and with overlapping terms, should have an independent voice to speak out on the problems confronting the state's child protection system. [See section 22.]

Central Register of Child Protection Cases

Over forty states have established a central register of child protection cases. If designed and operated correctly, a central register can help child protective workers assess the danger to a child they suspect is being abused or neglected. By helping to locate previous reports on the same child or his siblings, the central register can be invaluable in determining whether there is a repeating or continuing pattern of parental maltreatment. The repetition of suspicious injuries is strongly indicative of child abuse, and only through a central register or some other kind of central indexing of information can such information be gathered and

---

*This provision is primarily targeted to "state supervised" systems, in which counties operate the child protection program, as opposed to "state administered" systems.

reviewed. Because families in such cases often go from hospital to hospital or social service agency to social service agency, the only way a physician or protective worker can quickly know whether a prior report has been made is through a central register of reports.

Perhaps equally as important, a central register can help ensure that investigations are properly performed and services provided. If it can receive and process reports immediately and can review them for their timeliness, it can monitor the provision of services on an ongoing and continuing basis. The central register can also be used as a research tool to determine the incidence of reported abuse and neglect in a state and the most effective types of treatment. [See section 21.]

Confidentiality and the Right to Privacy of Those Reported

Many of the reports kept by the child protective service, or stored and made easily accessible by the central register, prove to be unfounded. Sometimes they are made by malicious neighbors or relatives; more often reporters, though well-intentioned, are mistaken in their suspicions. Under the Model Act, no data on a family can be kept in the register if the report turns out to be "unfounded"; all unfounded reports are removed from the register. Even when the reports in the register are valid, there is still a need to protect the rights and sensibilities of those who are named in them. For, these records contain information about the most private aspects of personal and family life. Improper disclosure could stigmatize the future of all those mentioned in the report. Therefore, access to data in the register is carefully limited to those professionals and officials who are responsible for making emergency decisions to protect endangered children. The data in the register is made confidential; its unlawful use is a crime. [See sections 21(f) and 24.]

As a matter of fundamental fairness, people ought to know what information a government agency is keeping about them. The Model Act guarantees the subject of a report the right to see all the information about him in the report or register at any time. Nevertheless, the subject of the report's right to access is not absolute. The identity of any person who made the report or who cooperated with the subsequent investigation may be withheld when giving such information "likely to be detrimental to the safety or interests of such person."

Furthermore, the subject of a report may use his or her knowledge of what is in the report to request the state department to amend, expunge, or remove the record from the register. If the state department does not do so, the subject has a right to a "fair hearing" similar to those held to determine whether a recipient's public assistance can be terminated. [See section 21(i).]

Institutional Child Abuse and Neglect

Unfortunately, children are sometimes abused and neglected by the very institutions meant to protect them from harm.

The Model Act seeks to deal with those situations in which children are abused while living in public and private *residential* facilities. It provides for an independent investigation of all reports of institutional abuse and neglect; no agency should be allowed to investigate itself when a report of institutional abuse and neglect has been made. An outside, disinterested agency must perform this investigation. [See section 23.]

Right to Counsel in Child Protective Proceedings

Court proceedings involving child abuse and child neglect can have profoundly important consequences for the children and parents involved. Children can be removed from their parents and placed in foster care or institutions for months or years, even until they reach their majority. Moreover, the involuntary intrusion into the family by the court and related social agencies can be unpleasant and traumatic to all involved. Therefore, the Model Act seeks to protect the right of parents and children to a full and fair judicial review before intrusion into family life is authorized by a court. Both the parents and the children must be provided with legal counsel to represent them and their wishes before the court. [See section 25.]

In addition, the Model Act recognizes that the local child protective service also needs legal assistance in the presentation of information to the court. Therefore, the Model Act also requires that a child protective agency is also represented by counsel. [See section 25(c).]

Professional and Public Education

The key to real progress in the prevention, identification, and treatment of child abuse and neglect is the support of an informed and aware citizenry coupled with the capable efforts of concerned professionals. Therefore, the last major section of the Model Act requires a comprehensive and continuing state *and* local program of education and training for the general public and professionals, including child protective workers. [See section 26.]

Education programs should include general information on child abuse and neglect, as well as specific information on the law, reporting procedures and the child protective system. An effort should also be made to reach parents who may need help—to let them know they are not alone and where they can get help.

IMPLEMENTING THE MODEL ACT

The law embodied in the Model Act is an essential first step in the development of a community network of prevention and treatment services. As a totality, this system may look like an impossible ideal, but each of its elements has been tried and found effective somewhere in the United States. Based on the research and experience of professionals in the field, the Model Act's provisions form the basis of an effective and fair child protective system.

A law lives in the way it is used, however. Without the dedicated support of those who must implement it, even the most far-reaching, well-intentioned law is useless. Any state considering adoption of the Model Act, in whole or part, should do so only after the broadest possible consultation with child protective professionals and the public. Those affected by the law have to be involved in its development if they are going to accept the law and work to fulfill its provisions.

Moreover, no law is the ultimate answer to any problem. A law may prohibit child abuse and neglect, but it cannot prevent or cure it. A law may mandate the treatment of parents, but it cannot rehabilitate them. A law can establish the institutional framework for the protection of children, and it can enunciate the philosophy that will motivate and guide a system as it deals with the individual problems of children and families. Ultimately, the prevention and treatment of child abuse and child neglect depend less on laws and more on the existence of sufficient and suitable helping services for children and parents.

Chapter 8

MODEL CHILD PROTECTION ACT

SECTION 1. TITLE

This Act shall be known as the Child Protective Services Act of
19••.

SECTION 2. FINDINGS AND PURPOSE

Abused and neglected children in this state urgently need protection.
It is the purpose of this Act to help save them from further injury and
harm. This Act seeks to establish a fair and effective state and local child
protection system by providing those procedures and services necessary
to safeguard the well-being and development of endangered children
and to preserve and stabilize family life, whenever appropriate. Recognizing that children also can be abused and neglected while living in public
and private residential agencies and institutions meant to serve them,
this Act also provides for the appropriate handling of reports of institutional
child abuse and neglect.

SECTION 3. PERSONS OR FAMILIES NEEDING
ASSISTANCE ENCOURAGED TO SEEK IT

Any person or family seeking assistance in meeting child care responsibilities may use, and is encouraged to use, the services and facilities
established by this Act, including the single statewide telephone number
and the local child protective service. Whether or not the problem
presented constitutes child abuse or neglect as defined by this Act, such
persons or families shall be referred to appropriate community resources
or agencies. No person seeking assistance under this section shall be
required to give his name or any other identifying information.

SECTION 4. DEFINITIONS

When used in this Act and unless the specific context indicates otherwise:

(a) "Child" means a person under the age of 18.

(b) An "abused or neglected child" means a child whose physical or mental health or welfare is harmed or threatened with harm by the acts or omissions of his parent or other person responsible for his welfare.

(c) "Harm" to a child's health or welfare can occur when the parent or other person responsible for his welfare:

  (i) Inflicts, or allows to be inflicted, upon the child, physical or mental injury, including injuries sustained as a result of excessive corporal punishment; or

  (ii) Commits, or allows to be committed, against the child, a sexual offense, as defined by state law; or

  (iii) Fails to supply the child with adequate food, clothing, shelter, education (as defined by state law), or health care, though financially able to do so or offered financial or other reasonable means to do so; for the purposes of this Act, "adequate health care" includes any medical or non-medical remedial health care permitted or authorized under state law; or

  (iv) Abandons the child, as defined by state law; or

  (v) Fails to provide the child with adequate care, supervision, or guardianship by specific acts or omissions of a similarly serious nature requiring the intervention of the child protective service or a court.

(d) "Threatened harm" means a substantial risk of harm.

(e) "A person responsible for a child's welfare" includes the child's parent; guardian; foster parent; an employee of a public or private residential home, institution or agency; or other person legally responsible for the child's welfare in a residential setting.

(f) "Physical injury" means death, or permanent or temporary disfigurement or impairment of any bodily organ.

(g) "Mental injury" means an injury to the intellectual or psychological capacity of a child as evidenced by an observable and substantial impairment in his ability to function within his normal range of performance and behavior, with due regard to his culture.

(h) "Institutional child abuse and neglect" means situations of known or suspected child abuse or neglect where the person responsible for the child's welfare is a foster parent or the employee of a public or private residential home, institution, or agency.

(i) "State department" means the department designated under section 19 to have prime responsibility for state efforts to strengthen and improve the prevention, identification and treatment of child abuse and neglect.

(j) "Subject of the report" means any person reported under this Act, including any child or parent, guardian, or other person responsible for the child's welfare.

(k) "Unfounded report" means a report made pursuant to this Act for which there is no probable cause to believe that the child is abused or neglected. For the purposes of this Act, it is presumed that all reports are unfounded unless the child protective service determines otherwise.

(l) "Probable cause" means facts and circumstances based upon accurate and reliable information (including hearsay) that would justify a reasonable person to believe that a child subject to a report under this Act is abused or neglected. Such facts and circumstances may include evidence of an injury or injuries, if not satisfactorily explained, and the statements of a person worthy of belief, even if there is no present evidence of injury.

Title II: Reporting Procedure and Initial Child Protective Actions

SECTION 5. PERSONS AND OFFICIALS REQUIRED TO KNOWN AND SUSPECTED CHILD ABUSE OR NEGLECT

(a) When the following professionals and officials know or have reasonable cause to suspect that a child known to them in their professional or official capacity is an abused or neglected child, they are required to report or cause a report to be made in accordance with this Act: any physician; resident; intern; hospital personnel engaged in the admission, examination, care or treatment of persons; nurse; osteopath; chiropractor; podiatrist; medical examiner or coroner; dentist; optometrist; or any other health or mental health professional; Christian Science practitioner; religious healer; school teacher or other school official or pupil personnel;

social worker, professional day care center or any other professional child care, foster care, residential, or institutional worker; or peace officer or other law enforcement official.

(b) Whenever a person is required to report under this Act in his capacity as a member of the staff of a medical or other public or private institution, school, facility, or agency, he shall immediately notify the person in charge, or his designated agent, who shall then become responsible to make the report or cause the report to be made. However, nothing in this section or Act is intended to relieve individuals of their obligation to report on their own behalf, unless a report already has been made or will be made forthwith.

SECTION 6. ANY PERSON PERMITTED TO REPORT

Any person may make a report under this Act, if he knows or has reasonable cause to suspect that a child is abused or neglected.

SECTION 7. MANDATORY REPORTING OF DEATHS TO AND POSTMORTEM INVESTIGATION BY MEDICAL EXAMINER OR CORONER

Any person or official required to report under this Act who has reasonable cause to suspect that a child has died as a result of child abuse or neglect shall report his suspicion to the appropriate medical examiner or coroner. Any other person who has reasonable cause to suspect that a child has died as a result of child abuse or neglect may report his suspicion to the appropriate medical examiner or coroner. The medical examiner or coroner shall investigate the report and submit his findings, in writing, to the local law enforcement agency, the appropriate district attorney, the local child protective service, and, if the institution making the report is a hospital, the hospital.

SECTION 8. PHOTOGRAPHS AND X–RAYS

Any person or official required to report under this Act may take, or cause to be taken, photographs of the areas of trauma visible on a child who is the subject of a report and, if medically indicated, cause to be performed a radiological examination of the child without the consent of the child's parents or guardians. Whenever such person is required to report in his capacity as a member of the staff of a medical or other public or private institution, school, facility, or agency, he shall immediately notify the person in charge, or his designated agent, who shall then take or cause to be taken color photographs of visible trauma and shall, if medically indicated, cause to be performed a radiological examination of the child. The reasonable cost of photographs or x-rays taken under this section shall be reimbursed by the appropriate local child protective service. All photographs and x-rays taken, or copies of them, shall be sent to the local child protective service at the time the written confirmation report is sent, or as soon thereafter as possible.

SECTION 9. PROTECTIVE CUSTODY

(a) A police or law enforcement official [*a designated worker of a child protective service,*]* and a physician treating a child may take a child into protective custody without the consent of parents, guardians, or others exercising temporary or permanent control over the child when (1) he has reasonable cause to believe that there exists an imminent danger to the child's life or safety, (2) the parents are unavailable or do not consent to the child's removal from their custody, and (3) there is not time to apply for a court order.

(b) The person in charge of any hospital or similar medical institution may retain custody of a child reasonably suspected of being abused or neglected, when he believes the facts so warrant, whether or not additional medical treatment is required and whether or not the parents or other person responsible for the child's welfare request the child's return.

(c) The child shall be taken to a place previously designated for this purpose by the juvenile court [*or family court or similar civil court*]† [*the local protective service*].‡ Such place may include a foster home; group home; shelter; hospital, if the child is or will be presently admitted to the hospital; or other institution; but it shall not be a jail or other place for the detention of criminal or juvenile offenders.

(d) No child shall be kept in protective custody under this Act for more than twenty-four hours unless authorized by a judge of a court of record.

---

*As appropriate.

†As appropriate.

‡Optional.

(e) Any person taking a child into protective custody shall immediately notify the appropriate local child protective service. Upon such notification, the service shall immediately see to the protection of any other children in the home, commence a child protective investigation in accordance with Section 16 of this Act, and make every reasonable effort to inform the parent or other person responsible for the child's welfare of the place to which the child has been taken. The service shall make a reasonable attempt to return the child to his home, whenever it seems safe to do so. At the next regular session of the juvenile court [*or family court or similar civil court*]*, the service shall (i) commence a child protection proceeding in the court, or (ii) recommend to the court [*court intake service or other initiating authority*]† that one not be commenced. The court may order the commencement of a proceeding even if the service recommends against doing so, if it finds that such a proceeding would be in the best interests of the child. If a proceeding is commenced, the service shall recommend whether or not the child should be returned to his parents or other person responsible for his welfare pending further court action.

SECTION 10. IMMUNITY FROM LIABILITY

Any person, official, or institution participating in good faith in any act authorized or required by this Act shall be immune from any civil or criminal liability which might otherwise result by reason of such action.

SECTION 11. ABROGATION OF PRIVILEGED COMMUNICATIONS

The privileged quality of communication between husband and wife and any professional person and his patient or client, except that between attorney and client, shall not apply to situations involving known or suspected child abuse or neglect and shall not constitute grounds for failure to report as required or permitted by this Act, failure to cooperate with the child protective service in its activities pursuant to this Act, or failure to give or accept evidence in any judicial proceeding relating to child abuse or neglect.

---

*As appropriate.

†Optional.

SECTION 12. PENALTIES FOR FAILURE TO REPORT OR ACT

Any person, official, or institution required by this Act to report known or suspected child abuse or neglect, or required to perform any other act, who knowingly and willfully fails to do so or who knowingly and willfully prevents another person acting reasonably from doing so shall be guilty of a misdemeanor and shall be civilly liable for the damages proximately caused by such failure or prevention.

SECTION 13. INITIAL REPORTING PROCEDURE; STATEWIDE TOLL–FREE TELEPHONE NUMBER

(a) All reports of known or suspected child abuse or neglect made pursuant to this Act shall be made immediately by telephone to the statewide child protection center on the single, statewide, toll-free telephone number established by this Act.* They shall then be immediately transmitted to the appropriate local child protective service, unless the appropriate local plan for child protective services† provides that oral reports should be made directly to the local child protective service.

(b) All reports made pursuant to this Act shall be confirmed in writing to the appropriate local child protective service on forms supplied by the state department within forty-eight hours of the initial telephone report. The local child protective service shall send to the state center copies of all written confirmation reports it receives within twenty-four hours of receipt, regardless of where the initial oral report was received. Written confirmation reports from persons not required to report by this Act may be dispensed with by the state department for good cause shown. Written reports from persons or officials required by this Act to report shall be admissible in evidence in any judicial proceeding relating to child abuse or neglect.

(c) Reports involving known or suspected institutional child abuse or neglect shall be made and received in the same manner as all other reports made pursuant to this Act.

---

*See Section 21(b), *infra.*

†See Subsection 16(c) and Section 18, *infra.*

Title III. Local Responsibilities

SECTION 14. DESIGNATION OF LOCAL AGENCY

In each county [*or comparable political subdivision or geographic area*] of the state, the local agency having prime responsibility for local efforts to strengthen and improve the prevention, identification, and treatment of child abuse and neglect shall be [*the local department of social services*] or [*a designated unit within the department, such as the child welfare service or a unified child protective service*] [*designated by the state department*] or [*designated by the appropriate local governing authority.*]

SECTION 15. POWERS, FUNCTIONS, AND DUTIES OF LOCAL AGENCY

(a) The local agency shall administer the child protective service and shall have prime local responsibility for strengthening and improving child abuse and neglect prevention and treatment efforts. To the fullest extent feasible, the local agency shall (i) encourage the cooperation and assistance of public, private, and parental organizations; (ii) serve as a local clearinghouse on programs and organizations providing or concerned with human services related to the prevention, identification, or treatment of child abuse or neglect; (iii) compile, publish, and disseminate public, professional, and staff educational and training materials and it shall provide training and technical assistance to appropriate local agencies, organizations, and individuals, either directly or indirectly; and (iv) seek and encourage the development of improved or additional programs and activities, the assumption of prevention and treatment responsibilities by additional agencies and organizations, and the coordination of existing programs and activities.

(b) Each local agency shall establish or designate a unit to act as the local child protective service to perform only those functions assigned to it by this Act and other laws, or that would further the purposes of this Act. The local child protective service shall have sufficient staff or sufficient qualifications to fulfill the purposes of this Act and shall be organized to maximize the continuity of responsibility, care, and service of individual workers toward individual children and families. In counties [*or comparable political subdivisions or geographic areas*] of sufficient size, the child protective service shall be a separate organizational unit singly administered and supervised within the local agency.

(c) To effectuate the purposes of this Act, the local agency, to the fullest extent feasible, shall cooperate with and shall seek the cooperation and involvement of all appropriate public and private agencies, including law enforcement agencies, courts of competent jurisdiction, and agencies, organizations, or programs providing or concerned with human services related to the prevention, identification, or treatment of child abuse or neglect. Such cooperation and involvement shall include joint consultation and services, joint planning, joint case management, joint public education and information services, utilization of each others' facilities, joint staff development and other training, and the creation of multidisciplinary case diagnostic, case handling, case management, and policy planning teams.*

(d) In the furtherance of its responsibilities under this Act and in accordance with the terms and conditions of the local plan for child protective services,† the local agency may purchase and utilize the services of any public or private agency if adequate provision is made for continuity of care and accountability. When services are purchased by the local agency pursuant to this Act, their cost shall be reimbursed by the state to the locality in the same manner and to the same extent as if the services were provided directly by the local agency.‡

(e) The local agency shall have such other powers, functions, and duties as are assigned to it by this Act, other laws, and administrative procedures.

SECTION 16. THE LOCAL CHILD PROTECTIVE SERVICE

(a) The local child protective service shall be capable of receiving reports of known or suspected child abuse or neglect twenty-four hours a day, seven days a week. If it appears that the immediate safety or well-being of a child is endangered, the family may flee or the child disappear, or the facts otherwise so warrant, the child protective service

---

*See section 16(e), *infra.*

†See section 18, *infra.*

‡This last sentence is not necessary if the local agency is a local office of a state administered social services department.

shall commence an investigation immediately, regardless of the time of day or night. In all other cases, a child protective investigation shall be commenced within twenty-four hours of receipt of the report. To fulfill the requirements of this section, the child protective service shall have the capability of providing or arranging for comprehensive emergency services to children and families at all times of the day or night.

(b) For each report it receives, the child protective service shall promptly perform an appropriately thorough child protective investigation to: (i) determine the composition of the family or household, including the name, address, age, sex, and race of each child named in the report, and any siblings or other children in the same household or in the care of the same adults, the parents or other persons responsible for their welfare, and any other adults in the same household; (ii) determine whether there is probable cause to believe that any child in the family or household is abused or neglected, including a determination of harm or threatened harm to each child, the nature and extent of present or prior injuries, abuse or neglect, and any evidence thereof, and a determination of the person or persons apparently responsible for the abuse or neglect; (iii) determine the immediate or long-term risk to each child if it remains in the existing home environment; and (iv) determine the protective, treatment, and ameliorative services that appear necessary to help prevent further child abuse or neglect and to improve the home environment and the parent's ability to adequately care for the children. The purpose of the child protective investigation shall be to provide immediate and long-term protective services to prevent further abuse or neglect and to provide, or arrange for, and coordinate and monitor treatment and ameliorative services necessary to safeguard and insure the child's well-being and development and, if possible, to preserve and stabilize family life.

(c) In counties where the local plan for child protective services provides that reports of known and suspected child abuse and neglect are to be made directly to the local child protective service, the local service shall operate the telephone facility in a manner consistent with that of the statewide child protection center. Specifically, the local telephone facility shall make reports to and receive reports from the statewide center, shall immediately obtain information concerning prior reports from the statewide center and make such information available to those authorized by this Act to have it, and shall refer self-reports or inappropriate reports to appropriate community resources or agencies.

The local telephone facility shall have sufficient staff of sufficient qualifications and sufficient telephonic facilities to fulfill the purposes and functions assigned to it by this Act, other laws, or administrative procedures.

(d) If the local plan for child protective services so authorizes, the child protective service may waive a full child protective investigation of reports made by agencies or individuals specified in the local plan if, after an appropriate assessment of the situation, it is satisfied that (i) the protective and service needs of the child and the family can be met by the agency or individual, (ii) the agency or individual agrees to attempt to do so, and (iii) suitable safeguards are established and observed. Suitable safeguards shall include a written agreement from the agency or individual to report periodically on the status of the family, a written agreement to report immediately to the local service at any time that the child's safety or well-being is threatened despite the agency's or individual's efforts, and periodic monitoring of the agency's or individual's efforts by the local service for a reasonable period of time.

(e) The child protective service shall convene one or more interdisciplinary "Child Protection Teams" to assist it in its diagnostic, assessment, service, and coordination responsibilities. The head of the child protective service* or his designee shall serve as the team's coordinator. Members of the team shall serve at the coordinator's invitation and shall include representatives of appropriate health, mental health, social service, and law enforcement agencies.

(f) If the local child protective service is denied reasonable access to a child by the parents or other persons and the local service deems that the best interests of the child so require, it shall seek an appropriate court order or other legal authority to examine and interview such child.

(g) If the child protective service determines that a child requires immediate or long term protection, either (1) through homemaker care, day care, casework supervision, or other services to stabilize the home environment, or (2) through foster care, shelter care, or other substitute care to remove the child from his parent's custody, such services first shall be offered for the voluntary acceptance of the parent or other person responsible for the child's welfare. If such services are refused and the child protective service deems that the best interests of the child so

---

*In areas in which there is not a separate child protective service, this sentence should begin: "The head of the local agency . . . "

require, the service shall seek an appropriate court order or other legal authority to protect the child.*

(h) After providing for the immediate protection of the child but prior to offering any services to a family, the child protective service shall forthwith notify the adult subjects of the report, in writing, of the existence of the report and their rights pursuant to this Act, including their right to refuse services and their right to obtain access to and amend, expunge, or remove reports in the central register of child protection cases. The service shall explain that it has no legal authority to compel the family to accept services; however, it may inform the family of the obligations and authority of the child protective service to petition the juvenile court to decide whether a child is in need of care and protection or to refer the case to the police, district attorney or criminal court.

(i) No later than sixty days after receiving the initial report, the child protective service shall determine whether the report is unfounded or not and report its findings forthwith to the central register on a form supplied by the state department; however, the statewide center may extend the period in which such determinations must be made in individual cases for up to thirty days, but such extensions shall only be made once and only upon good cause shown.

(j) If the local child protective service determines that there is not probable cause to believe that a child is abused or neglected, it shall close its protective case. However, if it appears that the child or family could benefit from other social services, the local service may suggest such services for the family's voluntary acceptance or refusal. If the family declines such services, the local service shall take no further action.

(k) If the local child protective service determines that there is probable cause to believe that a child is abused or neglected, based upon its determination of the protective, treatment, and ameliorative service needs of the child and family, the local service shall develop, with the family, an appropriate service plan for the family's voluntary acceptance or refusal. The local service shall comply with subsection (h) by explaining its lack of legal authority to compel the acceptance of services and may explain its concomitant authority to petition the juvenile court or refer the case to the police, district attorney, or criminal court.

---

*The police and, if authorized by the optional provision in section 9(a), the child protective service may take the child into protective custody.

(l) If the local child protective service determines that the best interests of a child require juvenile court or criminal court action because an appropriate service plan was rejected or because of any other appropriate reason, the local service may initiate a court proceeding or a referral to the appropriate court related service, police department, district attorney, or any combination thereof.

(m) The child protective service shall give telephone notice and immediately forward a copy of reports which involve the death of a child to the appropriate district attorney [or other appropriate law enforcement agency] and medical examiner or coroner. In addition, upon the prior written request of the district attorney or if the local service otherwise deems it appropriate, a copy of any or all reports made pursuant to this Act which allege criminal conduct shall be forwarded immediately by the child protective service to the appropriate district attorney.

(n) If a law enforcement investigation is also contemplated or is in progress, the child protective service shall attempt to coordinate its efforts and concerns with those of the law enforcement agency.

(o) In any juvenile or criminal court proceeding commenced by the child protective service or by any other individual or agency, the service shall assist the court during all stages of the court proceeding in accordance with the purposes of this Act, the juvenile court act, and the penal law.

(p) The local child protective service shall maintain a local child abuse and neglect index of all cases reported under this Act which can enable it to determine the location of case records and to monitor the timely and proper investigation and disposition of cases. The index shall include the information contained in the initial, progress, and final reports required under this Act, and any other appropriate information.

(q) The child protective service shall prepare and transmit to the statewide child protection center the initial, preliminary, progress, and final reports required by section 21 (e) of this Act.

(r) The child protective service may request and shall receive from any agency of the state, or any of its political subdivisions, and any other agency providing services under the local plan for child protective services such cooperation, assistance, and information as will enable it to fulfill its responsibilities under this section.

SECTION 17. THE COMMUNITY CHILD PROTECTION ADVISORY BOARD

(a) The appropriate local chief executive officer shall convene a "community child protection advisory board." Members of the board shall include representatives of local law enforcement agencies, the juvenile [or family] court, appropriate public, private, and parental organizations, and individuals of distinction in human services, law, and community life, broadly representative of all social and economic groups. The board shall have no less than five and no more than fifteen members, of which at least twenty percent shall be individuals of distinction not otherwise representing a public, private, or parental organization or group.

(b) The community child protection advisory board, both independently and in conjunction with the local agency and the local child protective service, shall assist in local efforts to improve the prevention, identification, and treatment of child abuse and neglect. The advisory board may meet at any time to consider any issue in relation to child abuse and neglect, may confer with any individuals, groups, and agencies, and may issue reports or recommendations on any subject it deems appropriate.

SECTION 18. THE LOCAL PLAN FOR CHILD PROTECTIVE SERVICES

(a) After consultation with the community child protection advisory board, local law enforcement agencies, the juvenile [or family or other similar civil] court, other relevant public, private, and parental organizations, and individuals of distinction in human services, law and community life, broadly representative of all social and economic sectors, each local agency shall prepare a local plan for child protective services every two years, to be approved by the community child protection advisory board and the state department.

(b) The local plan shall describe the local agency's implementation of this Act, including (i) the child protective service's organization, staffing, method of operations, and financing, (ii) the programs in effect or planned in connection with the enforcement or implementation of this Act and other child abuse and neglect laws, and (iii) the terms and conditions under which the local child protective service may waive a full child protective investigation pursuant to subsection 16 (d) of this Act.

(c) The plan may take effect no sooner than 90 days and no later than 150 days after its submission to the state department. The date of submission shall be determined by the state department, which may stagger the receipt of such plans throughout the year.

(d) A public hearing shall be held by the community child protection advisory board at least 30 days before the plan must be submitted to the state department for its approval or disapproval. The plan shall be made available to the public for review and comment for at least 60 days before the public hearing. The availability of the plan and the hearing shall be widely publicized within the county [or comparable political or geographic subdivisions.]

(e) The plan shall be submitted to the state department after approval by the community child protection advisory board or upon the certification of the local agency that, after all reasonable efforts, the local agency and the board were not able to develop a mutually agreeable plan, stating the reasons therefore. The board may append to any plan it does not approve a statement of its reasons for disapproval before it is submitted to the state department.

(f) Within 30 days of its receipt, the state department shall certify whether or not the local plan fulfills the purposes and the requirements of this Act. If it disapproves the local plan, the state department shall give the reasons therefore, in writing, and the local agency shall have forty-five days to submit an amended plan in compliance with subsections (a) and (e) of this section. The state department shall have thirty days to certify whether or not the amended plan fulfills the purposes and meets the requirements of this Act. If the state department again disapproves the plan, the local agency shall have an additional thirty days to submit an amended plan of its own. The state department shall have thirty days to certify whether or not the second amended plan fulfills the purposes and meets the requirements of this Act. If the state department again disapproves the plan, at any time thereafter, it may withhold state reimbursement for all or part of the local agency's activities. The state department's failure to certify approval or disapproval of a plan within the times set forth in this section shall be deemed an approval. Decisions of the state department under this section shall be subject to judicial review in the form and manner prescribed by the state civil procedure law.*

Title IV. State Responsibilities

SECTION 19. DESIGNATION OF STATE DEPARTMENT

The state department having prime responsibility for state efforts to strengthen and improve the prevention, identification, and treatment of child abuse and neglect shall be the State Department of _____.

SECTION 20. POWERS, FUNCTIONS, AND DUTIES OF THE STATE DEPARTMENT

(a) The state department shall serve as a state clearinghouse on programs and groups providing or concerned with human services related to the prevention, identification, or treatment of child abuse or neglect. It shall compile, publish, and disseminate public, professional, and staff educational and training materials and provide training and technical assistance, directly or indirectly. The department shall encourage the development of improved and additional state and local programs and activities; encourage the assumption of prevention and treatment responsibilities by additional agencies and groups; encourage the coordination of existing programs and activities; and conduct, support, or foster research and demonstration projects.

(b) The head of the state department shall convene a "state child abuse and neglect coordinating committee," to coordinate and assist state efforts to strengthen and improve child abuse and neglect prevention and treatment. The committee shall be chaired by the head of the state department, or his personal designee, and shall be composed of representatives from state agencies providing or concerned with human services related to the prevention, identification, or treatment of child abuse and neglect.

(c) At least 45 days before the beginning of the state's fiscal year, the state department shall prepare and transmit to the Governor and the

---

*The last two sentences of this section would be inappropriate in States in which the local child protection program is state administered.

Legislature an "annual state report on child abuse and neglect prevention and treatment." The annual report shall describe the specific measures adopted to implement the provisions of this Act, as well as the accomplishments and shortcomings of state and local efforts to prevent and treat child abuse and neglect. The report shall include a full statistical analysis of the status and outcome of cases reported to the statewide center, an evaluation of services offered to the children and families reported, its recommendations for additional legislation or services to fulfill the purposes of this Act, and any other information deemed relevant. Based upon materials prepared by the state department pursuant to Title XX of the Federal Social Security Act and Public Law 93-247, the annual report shall describe state and local efforts to develop, strengthen, and carry out child abuse and neglect efforts in the coming year. The annual report shall also include a section prepared by the statewide citizen's committee on child abuse and neglect* which contains its comments, recommendations, or any other information deemed relevant to child abuse and neglect prevention and treatment efforts.

(d) The state department shall adopt regulations and forms necessary to implement this Act upon 45 days public notice for review and comment. However, this period may be shortened if the head of the state department certifies, in writing, the existence of an urgent necessity to do so and gives the reason therefore.

(e) The state department may request and shall receive from any agency of the state, or any of its political subdivisions, any agency receiving public funds, or any other agency providing services under the local child protective services plan, such cooperation, assistance, and information as will enable the state department and local agencies to fulfill their responsibilities under this Act.

(f) The state department shall have such other powers, functions, and duties as are assigned to it by this Act, other laws, and administrative procedures.

---

*See section 22, *infra*.

SECTION 21. THE STATEWIDE CHILD PROTECTION CENTER AND THE CENTRAL REGISTER OF CHILD PROTECTION CASES

(a) The state department shall establish a "statewide child protection center." The center shall be a separate organizational unit, singly administered and supervised within the state department, with sufficient staff of sufficient qualifications and sufficient resources, including telephone facilities, to fulfill the purposes and functions assigned to it by this Act, other laws, or administrative procedures.

(b) There shall be a single statewide, toll-free telephone number within the statewide child protection center which all persons, whether or not mandated by law, may use to report known or suspected child abuse or neglect at any hour of the day or night, on any day of the week. Immediately upon receipt of such reports, the center shall transmit the contents of the report, either orally or electronically, to the appropriate local child protective agency. Any person or family seeking assistance in meeting child care responsibilities may use the statewide telephone number to obtain assistance or information in accordance with section 3 of this Act. Any other person may use the statewide number to obtain assistance or information concerning the handling of child protection cases.

(c) There shall be a central register of child protection cases maintained in the statewide center. Through the recording of initial, preliminary, progress, and final reports, the central register shall be operated in such a manner as to enable the center to: (i) immediately identify and locate prior reports or cases of child abuse or neglect; (ii) continuously monitor the current status of all child protection cases;* and (iii) regularly evaluate the effectiveness and existing laws and programs through the development and analysis of statistical and other information.

(d) Immediately upon receiving an oral or written report of known or suspected child abuse or neglect, the statewide center shall notify the local service of a previous report concerning a subject of the present report or other pertinent information. In addition, upon satisfactory identification procedures, to be established by regulation of the state department, any person or official legally authorized to have access to records relating to child abuse and neglect may request and shall be

---

*Optional, because the costs of receiving, recording, and monitoring progress reports may be beyond the resources of some states.

immediately provided the information requested in accordance with the requirements of this Act. However, no information shall be released unless it prominently states whether the report is "under investigation," "unfounded," "under care," or "closed," whichever the case may be. The names and other identifying data and the dates and the circumstances of any persons requesting or receiving information from the central register shall be entered in the register record.

(e) (i) The statewide center shall prepare, print, and distribute initial, preliminary, progress, and final reporting forms to each local child protective service. (ii) Initial written reports from the reporting source shall contain the following information to the extent known at the time the report is made: the names and addresses of the child and his parents or other persons responsible for his welfare; the child's age, sex, and race; the nature and extent of the child's abuse or neglect, including any evidence of prior injuries, abuse, or neglect of the child or his siblings; the names of the persons apparently responsible for the abuse or neglect; family composition, including names, ages, sexes, and races of other children in the home; the name of the person making the report, his occupation, and where he can be reached; the actions taken by the reporting source, including the taking of photographs and x-rays, placing the child in protective custody, or notifying the medical examiner or coroner; and any other information the person making the report believes might be helpful in the furtherance of the purposes of this Act. (iii) Preliminary reports from the local child protective service shall be made no later than seven days after receipt of an initial report and shall describe the status of the child protective investigation up to that time, including an evaluation of the present family situation and danger to the child or children, corrections or updating of the initial report, and actions taken or contemplated. (iv) Progress reports* from the local service shall be made at such regular intervals as the regulations of the state department establish, and shall describe the child protective services' plan for protective, treatment, or ameliorative services and the services accepted or refused by the family. (v) Final reports from the local service shall be made no later than 14 days after a case is determined to be unfounded or is closed for other reasons and shall describe the final disposition of the case, including an evaluation of the reasons and

---

*Progress reports are considered optional because the cost of operating a system to store and monitor them may be beyond the resources of some states.

circumstances surrounding the close of the case and the unmet needs of the child or family, and the causes thereof, including the unavailability or unsuitability of existing services, and the need for additional services.*
(vi) The foregoing reports may contain such additional information in the furtherance of the purposes of this Act as the state department, by regulation, may require. (vii) All of the foregoing reports shall also be required of the child protective service in cases in which the local service foregoes a full protective investigation pursuant to the local plan for child protective services and subsection 16(d) of this Act. (viii) For good cause shown, the local service may amend any report previously sent to the statewide center. (ix) Unless otherwise prescribed by this Act, the contents, form, manner, and timing of making the foregoing reports shall be established by regulation of the state department.

(f) All cases in the central register shall be classified in one of four categories: "under investigation," "unfounded," "under care," or "closed," whichever the case may be. All information identifying the subjects of an unfounded report shall be expunged from the register forthwith. Identifying information on all other records shall be removed from the register no later than five years after the case is closed. However, if another report is received involving the same child, his sibling or offspring, or a child in the care of the same adults, the identifying information may be maintained in the register until five years after the subsequent case or report is closed.

(g) The central register may contain such other information which the state department determines to be in furtherance of the purposes of this Act. At any time, the statewide center may amend, expunge, or remove from the central register any record upon good cause shown and upon notice to the subjects of the report and the local child protective service.

(h) Upon request, a subject of a report shall be entitled to receive a copy of all information contained in the central register pertaining to his case. Provided, however, that the statewide center is authorized to prohibit the release of data that would identify a person who, in good faith, made a report or cooperated in a subsequent investigation, when it reasonably finds that disclosure of such information would be likely to be detrimental to the safety or interests of such person; in addition, the center may seek a court order from a court of competent jurisdiction

---

*But *see* section 16(j), *supra*, which authorizes the child protective service to provide services to the child or family if they are otherwise in need of such services and voluntarily accept them.

prohibiting the release of any information which the court finds is likely to be harmful to the subject of the report.

(i) At any time subsequent to the completion of the investigation, but in no event later than sixty days after receipt of the report, at which time this Act contemplates that the investigation will have been completed, a subject of a report may request the state department to amend, expunge, or remove the record of the report from the register. If the state department refuses to do so or does not act within thirty days, the subject shall have the right to a fair hearing within the state department to determine whether the record of the report should be amended, expunged, or removed on the grounds that it is inaccurate or it is being maintained in a manner inconsistent with this Act. Such fair hearing shall be held within a reasonable time after the subject's request at a reasonable place and hour. The appropriate local child protective service shall be given notice of the fair hearing. In such hearings, the burden of providing the accuracy and consistency of the record shall be on the state department and the appropriate local child protective service. A juvenile court [*family court or similar civil court*] finding of child abuse or child neglect shall be presumptive evidence that the report was not unfounded. The hearing shall be conducted by the head of the state department or his designated agent, who is hereby authorized and empowered to order the amendment, expunction, or removal of the record to make it accurate or consistent with the requirements of this Act. The decision shall be made, in writing, at the close of the hearing, or within thirty days thereof, and shall state the reasons upon which it is based. Decisions of the state department under this section shall be subject to judicial review in the form and manner prescribed by the state civil procedure law.

(j) To the fullest extent possible, written notice of any amendment, expunction, or removal of any record made pursuant to this Act shall be served upon each subject of such report and the appropriate local child protective service. The service, upon receipt of such notice, shall take the appropriate similar action in regard to the local child abuse and neglect index and shall inform, for the same purpose, any other individuals or agencies which received such record pursuant to this Act or in any other manner. Nothing in this section is intended to require the destruction of case records.

SECTION 22. STATEWIDE CITIZEN'S COMMITTEE ON CHILD ABUSE AND NEGLECT

The Governor shall appoint the chairperson and members of a "statewide citizen's committee on child abuse and neglect" to consult with and advise the Governor, the state department, and the state child abuse and neglect coordinating committee. The committee shall be composed of individuals of distinction in human services, law, and community life, broadly representative of all social and economic communities across the state, who shall be appointed to three year staggered terms. The chairperson and members of the committee shall serve without compensation, although their travel and per diem expenses shall be reimbursed in accordance with standard state procedures. Under procedures adopted by the committee, it may meet at any time, confer with any individuals, groups, and agencies; and may issue reports or recommendations on any aspect of child abuse or neglect it deems appropriate.

Title V: General

SECTION 23. REPORTS OF INSTITUTIONAL CHILD ABUSE AND NEGLECT

(a) Through written agreement, the state department shall designate the public or private agency or agencies responsible for investigating reports involving known or suspected institutional child abuse or neglect. The designated agency or agencies must be other than and separately administered from the one involved in the alleged acts or omissions. Subject to the preceding limitation, the agency may be the state department, the local child protective service, a law enforcement agency, or another appropriate agency.

(b) The agreement shall describe the specific terms and conditions of the designation, including the manner in which reports of known or suspected institutional child abuse or neglect will be received through the single statewide telephone number, the manner in which such reports will be investigated, the remedial action which will be taken, and the manner in which the statewide child protection center will be kept fully informed of the progress, findings, and disposition of the investigation.

SECTION 24. CONFIDENTIALITY OF REPORTS AND RECORDS

(a) In order to protect the rights of the child, his parents, or guardians, all records concerning reports of non-institutional child abuse and neglect, including reports made to the state department, state center, state central register, local child protective services, and all records generated as a result of such reports, shall be confidential and shall not be disclosed except as specifically authorized by this Act or other applicable law. It shall be a misdemeanor to permit, assist, or encourage the unauthorized release of any information contained in such reports or records.

(b) No person, official, or agency shall have access to such records unless in furtherance of the purposes directly connected with the administration of this Act. Such persons, officials, agencies, and purposes for access include:

(i) a local child protective service in the furtherance of its responsibilities under this Act;

(ii) a police or law enforcement agency investigating a report of known or suspected child abuse or neglect;

(iii) a physician who has before him a child whom he reasonably suspects may be abused or neglected;

(iv) a person legally authorized to place a child in protective custody when such person requires the information in the report or record to determine whether to place the child in protective custody;

(v) an agency having the legal responsibility or authorization to care for, treat, or supervise a child or parent, guardian, or other person responsible for the child's welfare who is the subject of a report;

(vi) except in regard to harmful or detrimental information as provided in section 21(h), any subject of the report; if the subject of the report is a minor or is otherwise legally incompetent, his general guardian or guardian *ad litem;*

(vii) a court, upon its finding that access to such records may be necessary for the determination of an issue before such court; however, such access shall be limited to in camera inspection, unless the court determines that public disclosure of the information contained therein is necessary for the resolution of an issue then pending before it;

(viii) a grand jury, upon its determination that access to such records is necessary in the conduct of its official business;

    (ix) any appropriate state or local official responsible for administration, supervision, or legislation in relation to the prevention or treatment of child abuse or neglect when carrying out his official functions;

    (x) any person engaged in bona fide research purposes; provided, however, that no information identifying the subjects of the report shall be made available to the researcher unless it is absolutely essential to the research purpose, suitable provision is made to maintain the confidentiality of the data, and the head of the state department or local agency gives prior written approval.

(c) Upon request, a physician or the person in charge of an institution, school, facility or agency making a legally mandated report shall receive a summary of the findings of and actions taken by the local child protective service in response to his report. The amount of detail such summary contains shall depend on the source of the report and shall be established by regulations of the state department. Any other person making a report shall be entitled to learn the general disposition of such report.

(d) A person given access to the names or other information identifying the subjects of the report, except the subject of the report, shall not make public such identifying information unless he is a district attorney or other law enforcement official and the purpose is to initiate court action. Violation of this subsection shall be a misdemeanor.

(e) Nothing in this Act is intended to affect existing policies or procedures concerning the status of court and criminal justice system records.

SECTION 25. RIGHT TO REPRESENTATION IN COURT PROCEEDINGS

(a) Any child who is alleged to be abused or neglected in a juvenile court [*family or other similar civil court*] proceeding shall have independent legal representation in such proceeding. If independent legal representation is not available, the court shall appoint counsel to represent the child at public expense. The attorney representing a child under this section shall also serve as the child's guardian *ad litem* unless a guardian *ad litem* has been appointed by the appropriate court.

(b) Any parent or other person responsible for a child's welfare alleged to have abused or neglected a child in a civil or criminal proceeding shall be entitled to legal representation in such proceeding. If he is unable to afford such representation, the appropriate court shall appoint counsel to represent him at public expense.

(c) In every juvenile [*or family*] court proceeding concerning alleged child abuse or neglect in which it is a party, the local child protective service shall have the assistance of legal counsel [*provided by the local civil law officer of the appropriate county or comparable political subdivision or geographic area.*]

SECTION 26. EDUCATION AND TRAINING

Within the appropriation available, the state department and the local agency, both jointly and individually, shall conduct a continuing education and training program for state and local department staff, persons and officials required to report, the general public, and any other appropriate persons. The program shall be designed to encourage the fullest degree of reporting of known and suspected child abuse and neglect, including institutional abuse and neglect, and to improve communication, cooperation, and coordination among all agencies in the identification, prevention, and treatment of child abuse and neglect. The program shall inform the general public and professionals of the nature and extent of child abuse and neglect and of their responsibilities, obligations, powers, and immunity from liability under this Act. It should also include information on the diagnosis of child abuse and neglect and the roles and procedures of the local child protective service and the community child protection team, the statewide child protection center and central register, the juvenile court and of the protective, treatment, and ameliorative services available to children and their families. The program should also encourage parents and other persons having responsibility for the welfare of children to seek assistance on their own in meeting their child care responsibilities and encourage the voluntary acceptance of available services when they are needed. It should also include wide publicity and dissemination of information on the existence and number of the twenty-four hour, statewide, toll-free telephone service to assist persons seeking assistance and to receive reports of known and suspected abuse and neglect.

SECTION 27. SEPARABILITY

If any provision of this Act or the application thereof to any person or circumstances is held to be invalid, the remainder of the Act and the application of such provision to other persons or circumstances shall not be affected thereby.

SECTION 28. AUTHORIZATION FOR APPROPRIATIONS

There are hereby authorized to be appropriated such sums as may be necessary to effectuate the purposes of this Act.

SECTION 29. EFFECTIVE DATE

This Act shall take effect on _____.

REFERENCES

Adams, J. A.; Harper, K., Knudson, S., and Revilla, J.: Examination findings in legally confirmed child sexual abuse. *Pediatrics, 94(3):*310–317, 1994.

Adelson, L.: Slaughter of the innocents: a study for forty-six homicides in which the victims were children. *N Engl J Med, 264:*1345, 1961.

Alexander, R.; Crabbe, L., Sato, Y., et al.: Serial abuse in children who are shaken. *Am J Dis Child, 144:*58–60, 1990.

Alexander, R.; Sato, Y., Smith, W., and Bennett, T.: Incidence of impact trauma with cranial injuries ascribed to shaking. *Am J Dis Child, 144(6):*724–726, 1990.

Alexander, R. C.; Schor, D. P., and Smith, W. L. Jr.: Magnetic resonance imaging of intracranial injuries from child abuse. *J Pediatr, 109(6):*975–979, 1986.

Alfaro, J.: Helping Children overcome the effects of abuse and neglect, *Pediatr Ann, 13:*778, 1984.

Altman, D. H., and Smith, R. L.: Unrecognized trauma in infants and children. *J Bone Joint Surg (Amer), 42A:*407, 1960.

Amegauie, L.; Marzouk, O., et al.: Munchausen's Syndrome by Proxy: A warning for health professionals. *Br Med J, 293:*855–856, 1986.

Ards, S., and Harrell, A.: Reporting of child maltreatment: a secondary analysis of the National Incidence Surveys. *Child Abuse & Neglect, 17(3):*337–344, 1993.

Augarten, A.; Laufer, J., Szeinberg, A., Passwell, J.: Child abuse, osteogenesis imperfecta and the grey zone between them. *J Med; Clinical, Experimental & Theoretical, 24(2–3):*171–175, 1993.

Ayoub, C., and Pfeifer, D.: Burns as a manifestation of child abuse and neglect. *Am J Dis Child, 133:*910, 1979.

Bain, K.: The physically abused child. *Pediatrics, 31:*895, 1963.

Bakwin, H.: Multiple skeletal lesions in young children due to trauma. *J Pediatr, 49:*7, 1956.

Beeber, B., and Cunningham, N.: Fatal child abuse and sudden infant death syndrome (SIDS): a critical diagnostic decision. *Pediatrics, 93(3):*539–540, 1994.

Belsky, J.: Etiology of child maltreatment: a developmental-ecological analysis. *Psychological Bulletin, 114(3):*413–434, 1993.

Bergman, A. B.; Larsen, R. M., and Mueller, B. A.: Changing spectrum of serious child abuse. *Pediatrics, 77:*113–116, 1986.

Besharov, Douglas J.: Contending with overblown expectations. *Public Welfare, 45(1):* 7–11, 1987.

Besharov, Douglas J.: The legal aspects of reporting known and suspected child abuse and neglect. *Villanova Law Review, 23(3):* 458–520, 1978.

Billmore, E. M., and Meyers, P. A.: Serious heart injury in infants: accident or abuse? *Pediatrics, 75:*340–342, 1985.

Bruce, D. A., and Zimmerman, R. A.: Shaken impact syndrome. *Pediatr Ann, 18:*482–494, 1989.

Budenz, Donald, et al.: Ocular and optic nerve hemorrhages in abused infants with intracranial injuries. *Ophthamology,* 101, *3:*559–565, 1994.

Caffey, J.: Multiple fractures in the long bones of infants suffering from chronic subdural hematoma. *AJR, 56:*163–173, 1946.

Caffey, J.: The whiplash shaken infant syndrome: manual shaking by the extremities with whiplash-induced intracranial and intraocular bleeding is linked with residual permanent brain damage and mental retardation. *Pediatrics, 54:*396–403, 1974.

Campbell, J. C.: Child abuse and wife abuse: the connections. *Maryland Medical Journal, 43(4):*349–350, 1994.

Cappelleri, J. C.; Eckenrode, J., and Powers, J. L.: The epidemiology of child abuse: findings from the Second National Incidence and Prevalence Study of Child Abuse and Neglect. *Am J of Public Health, 83(11):*1622–1624, 1993.

Carty, H. M.: Fractures caused by child abuse. *J of Bone & Joint Surgery, Br Volume, 75(6):*849–857, 1993.

Cohen, M. E. et al.: Psychological aspects of the maltreatment syndrome of childhood. *J Pediatr, 69:*279, 1966.

Crenshaw, W. B.; Bartell, P. A., and Lichtenberg, J. W.: Proposed revisions to mandatory reporting laws: an exploratory survey of child protective service agencies. *Child Welfare, 73(1):*15–27, 1994.

Daro, D., and McCurdy, K.: Preventing child abuse and neglect: programmatic interventions. *Child Welfare, 73(5):*405–430, 1994.

Davis, G. R.; Domoto, P. K., and Levy, R. L.: The dentist's role in child abuse and neglect: issues, identification and management. *J Dent Child, 46:*185–192, 1979.

Dees, D. N.: Child abuse by poisoning. *South Dakota Journal of Medicine, 46(3):*91–92, 1993.

DePanfilis, D., and Scannapieco, M.: Assessing the safety of children at risk of maltreatment: decision-making. *Child Welfare, 73(3):*229–245, 1994.

Devlin, B. K., and Reynolds, E.: Child Abuse. How to recognize it, how to intervene. *Am J Nursing, 94(3):*26–31, 1994.

Dine, M.: Intentional poisoning of children: an overlooked category of child abuse. *Pediatrics, 72:*16–21, 1983.

Dine, M. S.: Tranquilizer poisoning: an example of child abuse. *Pediatrics, 36:*782, 1965.

Dubowitz, H.: Medical neglect: what can physicians do? *Maryland Med J, 43(4):*337–341, 1994.

Edwards, A., et al.: Failure to thrive in early childhood. *Arch Dis Child, 62:*1263, 1990.

Ellerstein, N. S., and Norris, K. J.: Value of radiologic skeletal survey in assessment of abused children. *Pediatrics, 74:*1075–1078, 1984.

Elmer, E., et al.: Developmental characteristics of abused children. *Pediatrics 40,* 596, 1967.

Eisenstein, E. M.; Delta, B. G., and Clifford, J. H.: Jejunal hematoma: an unusual manifestation of the battered child syndrome. *Clin Pediatr, 4:*436, 1965.

Emery, J. L.: Child abuse, sudden infant death syndrome, and unexpected infant death. *Am J Dis Child, 147(10),* 1993.

Failure to thrive: Guides for record review. Supplement to *Pediatrics in Review,* American Academy of Pediatrics, 1993.

Feldman, K. W., and Brewer, D. K.: Child Abuse, Cardiopulmonary Resuscitation and Rib Fractures. *Pediatrics, 73:*339–342, 1984.

Finkelhor, D., and Dziuba-Leatherman, J.: Children as victims of violence: a national survey. *Pediatrics, 94(4 Pt 1):*413–420, 1994.

Fontana, V. J.: The maltreatment syndrome in children. *N Engl J Med, 269:*1389, 1963.

Fontana, V. J.: The neglect and abuse of children. *N Y State J Med, 64:*215, 1964.

Fontana, V. J.: An insidious and disturbing medical entity. *Public Welfare,* p. 235, July 1966.

Fontana, V. J.: Further reflections on maltreatment of children. *N Y State J Med, 68:*2214, 1968.

Fontana, V. J., and Robison, E.: A multidisciplinary approach to the treatment of child abuse. *Pediatrics, 57:*760–764, 1976.

Fontana, V. J., and Robison, E.: Observing child abuse. *J Pediatr,* 105, *4:*655–660, 1984.

Fowler, F. V.: The physician, the battered child and the law. *Pediatrics, 31:*488, 1963.

Frank, D., and Zeisel, S.: Failure to thrive. *Ped Clin North Am, 35:*1187, 1988.

Frauenberger, G. S., and Lis, E. F.: Multiple fractures associated with subdural hematoma in infancy. *Pediatrics, 6:*890, 1950.

Garbarino, J.: Psychological child maltreatment. A developmental view. *Primary Care, 20(2):*307–315, 1993.

Green, A. H.: Child sexual abuse: immediate and long-term effects and intervention. *J Am Academy of Child & Adolescent Psychiatry, 32(5):*890–902, 1993.

Green, M. A.; Clark, J. C., and Milroy, C. M.: Duty on child-abuse expert witnesses. *Lancet, 344(8931):*1231, 1994.

Guandolo, V. L.: Munchausen Syndrome by Proxy: an outpatient challenge. *Pediatrics, 75:*526–530, 1985.

Guidelines for the evaluation of sexual abuse in children. Committee on Child Abuse and Neglect. *American Academy of Pediatrics, Pediatrics, 87(2):*254–260, 1991.

Gwinn, J. L.; Lewis, K. W., and Peterson, H. G., Jr.: Roentgenorgraphic manifestations of unsuspected trauma in infancy. *J A M A, 1976:*926, 1961.

Hanson, R. M.: Sexually transmitted diseases and the sexually abused child. *Current Opinion in Pediatrics, 5(1):*41–49, 1993.

Hay, T., and Jones, L.: Societal interventions to prevent child abuse and neglect. *Child Welfare, 73(5):*379–403, 1994.

Hight, D. W.; Bakalar, H. R., and Lloyd, J. R.: Inflicted burns in children. *J A M A, 242:*517–570, 1979.

Hobbs, C. J.: Skull fracture and the diagnosis of abuse. *Arch Dis Child, 59:*246–252, 1984.

Hobbs, C. J., and Wynne, J. M.: The sexually abused battered child. *Arch Dis Child,* *65:*423–427, 1990.

Hunter, R. S., and Kilstrom, N.: Breaking the cycle in abusive families. *Am J Psychiatry, 136:*1320–1322, 1979.

Kemp, A. M.; Mott, A. M., and Sibert, J. R.: Accidents and child abuse in bathtub submersions. *Arch Dis Child, 70(5):*435–438, 1994.

Kempe, C. H.: Approaches to preventive child abuse. *The Health Visitors Concept, 130:*941–947, 1976.

Kempe, C. H.: Uncommon manifestations of the battered child syndrome. *Am J Dis Child, 129(11):*1265, 1975.

Kempe, C. H.; Silverman, F. N., Steele, B. F., et al.: The battered child syndrome. J A M A, 181:17–24, 1962.

Koel, B. S.: Failure to thrive and fatal injury as a continuum. *Am J Dis Child, 118:*565, 1969.

Leonidas, J. G.: Skeletal trauma in child abuse syndrome. *Pediatr Ann, 12(12):*875–874, 1983.

Leventhal, J. M.; Thomas, S. A., Rosenfield, N. S., and Markowitz, R. I.: Fractures in young children. Distinguishing child abuse from unintentional injuries. *Am J Dis Child, 147(1):*87–92, 1993.

Ludwig, S.: Shaken baby syndrome, a review of twenty cases. *Ann Emerg Med, 13:*104–107, 1984.

Malinosky-Rummell, R., and Hansen, D. J.: Long-term consequences of childhood physical abuse. *Psychological Bulletin, 114(1):*68–79, 1993.

Oliver, J. E.: Intergenerational transmission of child abuse: rates, research, and clinical implications. *Am J Psychiatry, 150(9):*1315–1324, 1993.

Paradise, J. E.: The medical evaluation of the sexually abused child. *Pediatr Clin North Am, 37:*839–862, 1990.

Pardess, E.; Finzi, R., and Sever, J.: Evaluating the best interests of the child—a model of multidisciplinary teamwork. *Medicine & Law, 12(3–5):*205–211, 1993.

Pascoe, J. M.; Hildebrandt, H. M., et al.: Patterns of skin injury in non-accidental and accidental injury. *Pediatrics, 64:*245, 1979.

Paterson, C. R.; Burns, J., and McAllion, S. J.: Osteogenesis imperfecta: the distinction from child abuse and the recognition of a variant form. *Am J Med Genetics, 45(2):*187–192, 1993.

Reece, R. M.: Fatal Child abuse and sudden infant death syndrome: a critical diagnostic decision. *Pediatrics, 91:*423–429, 1993.

Reece, R. M., and Grodon, M. A.: Recognition of non-accidental injury. *Pediatr Clin North Am, 32:*41–60, 1985.

Renz, B. M., and Sherman, R.: Abusive scald burns in infants and children: a prospective study. *American Surgeon, 59(5):*329–334, 1993.

Rosenberg, D.: Web of deceit: a literature review of Munchausen Syndrome by Proxy. *Child Abuse Negl, 11:*547, 1987.

Sandler, A. P., and Haynes, V.: Non-accidental trauma and medical folk belief, a case of cupping. *Pediatrics, 61:*921–922, 1978.

Sato, Y.; Yuh, W. T. C., Smith, W. L., et al.: MRI evaluation of head injury in child abuse. *Radiology, 173:*653–657, 1989.

Schnads, Y.; Frand, M., Rotem, Y., et al.: The chemically abused child. *Pediatrics, 68:*119, 1981.

Silver, H. K., and Kempe, C. H.: The problem of parental criminal neglect and severe physical abuse of children. *Am J Dis Child, 98:*528, 1959.

Silverman, F. N.: The roentgen manifestations of unrecognized skeletal trauma in infants. *Am J Roentgenol Radium Ther Nucl Med, 69:*413, 1953.

Sinal, S. H., and Ball, M. R.: Head trauma due to child abuse: serial computerized tomography in diagnosis and management. *South Med J, 80:*1505–1512, 1987.

Sivit, C. J.; Taylor, G. A., and Eichelberger, M. R.: Visceral injury in battered children: a changing perspective. *Radiology, 173:*659–661, 1989.

Skuse, D. H.: Non-organic failure to thrive: a reappraisal. *Arch Dis Child, 60:*173, 1985.

Soderstrom, R. M.: Colposcopic documentation. An objective approach to assessing sexual abuse of girls. *J of Reproductive Medicine, 39(1):*6–8, 1994.

Stevens-Simon, C., and Reichert, S.: Sexual abuse, adolescent pregnancy, and child abuse. A developmental approach to an intergenerational cycle. *Arch of Pediatrics & Adolescent Medicine, 148(1):*23–27, 1994.

Tipton, A. C.: Child sexual abuse: physical examination techniques and interpretation of findings. *Adolesc Pediatr Gynecol, 2:*10–25, 1989.

Urquiza, A. J.; Wirtz, S. J., Peterson, M. S., and Singer, V. A.: Screening and evaluating abused and neglected children entering protective custody. *Child Welfare, 73(2):*155–171, 1994.

Warner, J. E., and Hansen, D. J.: The identification and reporting of physical abuse by physicians: a review and implications for research. *Child Abuse Negl, 18:*11–25, 1994.

Wells, S. J.: Child protective services: research for the future. *Child Welfare, 73(5):*431–447, 1994.

White, S. T.; Loda, F. A., Ingnam, D. L., et al.: Sexually transmitted diseases in sexually abused children. *Pediatrics, 72:*16–21, 1983.

Wilkinson, W. S.; Han, D. P., Rappley, M. D., et al.: Retinal hemorrhage predicts neurologic injury in the shaken baby syndrome. *Arch Ophthalmol, 107(10):*1472–1474, 1989.

Woolley, P. V., Jr., and Evans, W. A., Jr.: Significance of skeletal lesions in infants resembling those of traumatic origin. *J A M A, 158:*539, 1955.

Zuravin, S. J.; Benedict, M., and Somerfield, M.: Child maltreatment in family foster care. *Am J Orthopsychiatry, 63(4):*589–596, 1993.

SELECTED RESOURCES

Books

Accardo, P. J. (Ed.): *Failure to Thrive in Infancy and Early Childhood.* Baltimore, University Park Press, 1982.

Arnold, L. Eugene (Ed.): *Helping Parents Help their Children.* New York, Brunner/Mazel, 1978.

Barbero, G. J.; Morris, M. G., and Redford, M. T.: *The Neglected-Battered Child Syndrome: Role Reversal in Parents.* New York, Child Welfare League of America, 1963.

Besharov, Douglas J.: *Recognizing Child Abuse: A Guide for the Concerned.* New York, Free Press, 1990.

Besharov, Douglas J.: *Protecting Children From Abuse and Neglect: Policy and Practice.* Springfield, Charles C Thomas, 1988.

Fontana, Vincent J.: *Save the Family, Save the Child.* New York, Dutton (hard cover), 1991, Mentor (paperback), 1992.

Kempe, C. H., and Kempe, R. S.: *Child Abuse.* Cambridge, Harvard University Press, 1978.

Kempe, C. Henry, and Helfer, Ray E. (Eds.): *Helping the Battered Child and His Family.* Philadelphia, Lippincott, 1972.

Kempe, C. Henry, and Helfer, Ray E. (Eds.): *Child Abuse and Neglect: The Family and the Community.* Cambridge, Ballinger, 1976.

Monteleone, James A., and Brodeur, Armand E.: *Child Maltreatment: A Clinical Guide and Reference.* St. Louis, G. W. Medical Publishing, Inc., 1994.

Reece, R. M. (Ed.): *Child Abuse: Medical Diagnosis and Management.* Malvern, Lea and Febiger, 1993.

Schetky, Diane H., Green, Arthur H.: *Child Sexual Abuse: A Handbook for Health Care and Legal Professionals.* New York, Brunner/Mazel, 1988.

Information Centers:

The American Humane Association, Children's Division, 63 Inverness Drive East, Englewood, Colorado 80112.

C. Henry Kempe Center for Prevention and Treatment of Child Abuse and Neglect, 1205 Oneida Street, Denver, Colorado 80220.

Child Welfare League of America, 440 1st Street, N. W., Suite 310, Washington, D. C. 20001.

Childhelp USA, 1345 El Centro, Hollywood, California 90028.

National Committee for Prevention of Child Abuse, 332 South Michigan Avenue, Chicago, Illinois 60604.

The National Clearinghouse on Child Abuse and Neglect Information, P.O. Box 1182, Washington, D. C. 20013-1182.

AUTHOR INDEX

149

SUBJECT INDEX